Flask API for Mobile App Development

No more feeling overwhelmed – you'll be a Flask whiz in no time!
Kiss Complex Frameworks Goodbye! The Lightweight Path to
Building Powerful Backends and more!

Katie Millie

Flask API for Mobile App Development

No more feeling overwhelmed – you'll be a Flask whiz in no time! Kiss Complex Frameworks Goodbye! The Lightweight Path to Building Powerful Backends and more!

By

Katie Millie

Copyright notice

Copyright © 2024 Katie Millie. All rights reserved.

No portion of this work by Katie Millie may be reproduced, distributed, or transmitted in any form or by any means—whether electronic, mechanical, photocopying, recording, or otherwise—without the prior written consent of the author. This restriction applies except for brief quotations used in critical reviews and specific noncommercial purposes allowed by copyright law. Unauthorized use, duplication, or dissemination of this material, in part or in whole, is strictly forbidden and will result in legal action.

Katie Millie dedicates substantial effort to creating unique and captivating content, making the protection of her intellectual property essential. If you wish to use any part of this work for educational, scholarly, or other purposes beyond what is legally permitted, please contact the author to obtain permission. By adhering to these guidelines, you support the creative process and help ensure that Katie Millie can continue to produce valuable and inspiring work. Thank you for your cooperation and understanding.

Table of Contents

INTRODUCTION
Chapter 1
    Why Flask for Mobile App Development?
        Setting Up Your Flask Development Environment for Mobile App Development
            Your First Flask Application - Hello, World!
                Understanding Flask's Core Components (Routes, Views, Templates)
Chapter 2
    Demystifying RESTful Architecture - Principles and Benefits
        Designing Powerful RESTful Endpoints for Your Mobile App
            Handling HTTP Methods (GET, POST, PUT, DELETE) in Flask for Mobile App Development
                Building a Clean API Structure with Blueprints in Flask for Mobile App Development
Chapter 3
    Working with Data in Flask: Requests, Responses, and JSON
        Integrating Databases with Flask (Popular Options and Connection)
            CRUD Operations (Create, Read, Update, Delete) with Flask and Databases

User Authentication and Authorization for Secure Data Access in Flask API

Chapter 4

Security Sentinel - Guarding Your Mobile App Fortress

Authorization Strategies: Role-Based Access Control (RBAC) in Flask API for Mobile App Development

Securing API Endpoints from Malicious Attacks in Flask for Mobile App Development

Data Encryption and Security Considerations for Mobile Apps Using Flask API

Chapter 5

Why Testing Matters: Unit Testing and Integration Testing for Flask API in Mobile App Development

Setting Up a Testing Environment for Flask Applications

Testing Flask Routes, Views, and Database Interactions

Writing Clean and Maintainable Code with Unit Tests for a Flask API in Mobile App Development

Chapter 6

Choosing a Deployment Strategy: On-premise vs. Cloud Options for Flask APIs in Mobile App Development

Deploying Your Flask API to Production Environments

Scalability Considerations for High Traffic Mobile Apps

Monitoring and Maintaining Your

Deployed Flask API

Chapter 7

Flask in Action - Inspiring Examples of Mobile Apps

Crafting a Location-Based Service with Flask and Geolocation

Designing a Real-Time Chat Application with Flask APIs

Exploring Additional Mobile App Use Cases with Flask

Chapter 8

Using Flask Extensions for Enhanced Functionality (Security, Serialization)

Working with Asynchronous Tasks and Background Jobs

Leveraging Caching Mechanisms for Improved Performance

Best Practices for Error Handling and Logging in Flask APIs

Chapter 9

The Future of Flask Mobile App Development

Integrating Flask APIs with Cloud Services (AWS, Google Cloud)

Continuous Integration and Continuous Delivery (CI/CD) for Flask Apps

Staying Updated: Resources for Flask Developers

Conclusion

Appendix

Glossary of terms

Essential Flask Resources and Libraries

Common Flask API Development Pitfalls and Solutions

INTRODUCTION

From Flask to Freedom - Building Mobile Apps You Love (Without the Heavies)

Imagine this: you have a brilliant idea for a mobile app. It's sleek, innovative, and poised to revolutionize the way people [insert your app's function here]. But then reality hits. The complex frameworks, the endless lines of code, the feeling of being lost in a developer jungle. Suddenly, your dream app starts to feel like a distant mirage.

Fear not, fellow app adventurer! There's a hidden path through the developer jungle, a path paved with clarity,efficiency, and, most importantly, **fun**. This path leads straight to **Flask**, the Python web framework that empowers you to build powerful mobile app APIs without the weight of heavyweight frameworks.

Flask API for Mobile App Development is your friendly guide on this exciting journey. Forget the intimidation factor – this book is written in a clear and engaging style, packed with practical examples and code snippets you can understand and use immediately. It's your roadmap to building robust mobile app backends using the power of Python and Flask.

Here's a sneak peek at the treasures you'll unearth within these pages:

- **Flask Fundamentals for the Win:** We'll break down Flask's core concepts into bite-sized pieces, ensuring a smooth learning curve even if you're new to Python web development. No more feeling overwhelmed – you'll be a Flask whiz in no time!
- **API Alchemy:** Transform Flask into a mobile app development powerhouse. Learn how to design elegant and secure RESTful APIs that seamlessly communicate with your mobile app, ensuring smooth data flow and exceptional user experiences.
- **Data Dance:** Master the art of data management. Explore how to handle user data, process information, and integrate with databases to fuel your mobile app with the functionality it needs to thrive.
- **Authentication Adventure:** Become a guardian of your app's security. Discover best practices for user authentication and authorization, ensuring your app remains a safe haven for your users' data.
- **Testing Titans:** Build bulletproof APIs with confidence. Learn the power of unit testing and integration testing to guarantee your backend functions flawlessly, saving you frustration down the line.
- **Deployment Dynasty:** Launch your mobile app with a flourish. Explore different deployment strategies, from on-premise solutions to cloud-

based deployments, to ensure your app reaches the world and ignites user engagement.
- **Real-World Inspiration:** Let creativity take flight. Explore captivating real-world scenarios where Flask APIs power incredible mobile apps. From building interactive social media platforms to crafting location-based services, the possibilities are endless.

Flask API for Mobile App Development is more than just a technical manual – it's your launchpad to mobile app development freedom. Forget the limitations of complex frameworks and embrace the agility and efficiency of Flask. This book empowers you to:

- **Build APIs in record time:** Focus on the core functionality of your mobile app, not wrestling with cumbersome frameworks. Flask's lightweight nature allows you to iterate and innovate at lightning speed.
- **Write clean and maintainable code:** Learn Flask's best practices for structuring your projects for optimal readability and future development.
- **Deliver exceptional user experiences:** Craft mobile app backends that are secure, efficient, and empower your app to provide a seamless and enjoyable experience for your users.

Are you ready to:

- **Break free from the limitations of complex frameworks?**

- **Build mobile apps faster and more efficiently?**
- **Become a master of Flask API development?**

Join the Flask revolution and turn your mobile app dreams into reality. **Get your copy of Flask API for Mobile App Development today and unlock the power to build incredible mobile applications, all on your own terms!**

Chapter 1

Why Flask for Mobile App Development?

Flask is a lightweight, flexible, and robust web framework for Python. It's a popular choice for backend development, particularly for creating RESTful APIs which can serve as the backbone for mobile applications. This essay explores the advantages of using Flask for mobile app development, demonstrates its implementation, and provides practical examples of how to build a Flask API for a mobile application.

Advantages of Using Flask

1. Simplicity and Flexibility: Flask is minimalistic and allows developers to add only the components they need, making it highly flexible. This is particularly useful for mobile app development where specific features are often required without the overhead of a full-stack framework.

2. Modularity: Flask supports modular programming, allowing developers to break down applications into smaller, manageable modules. This modularity is crucial for scaling mobile applications.

3. Extensive Documentation and Community Support: Flask has comprehensive documentation and a vibrant community, providing ample resources and support for developers. This can accelerate the development process and troubleshooting.

4. Integration Capabilities: Flask can easily integrate with various databases and third-party services, which is essential for mobile apps that require complex data handling and external service integrations.

5. Microservices Architecture: Flask is well-suited for microservices architecture, enabling the development of small, independently deployable services that communicate with each other. This architecture is ideal for mobile apps that need to scale efficiently.

Setting Up a Flask API for a Mobile App

Here's a step-by-step guide to setting up a basic Flask API that can be used for mobile app development:

1. Installation: First, you need to install Flask. You can do this using pip:

```bash
pip install Flask
```

```

**2. Creating a Simple Flask Application:** Create a new Python file (e.g., `app.py`) and set up a basic Flask application.

```python
from flask import Flask, jsonify, request

app = Flask(__name__)

@app.route('/')
def home():
    return "Welcome to the Flask API for Mobile App"

if __name__ == '__main__':
    app.run(debug=True)
```

3. Creating API Endpoints: To interact with the mobile app, we need to create RESTful API endpoints. Here's an example of creating a simple API for managing user data.

```python
users = []
```
```

```python
@app.route('/users', methods=['GET'])
def get_users():
    return jsonify(users)

@app.route('/users', methods=['POST'])
def add_user():
    new_user = request.get_json()
    users.append(new_user)
    return jsonify(new_user), 201

@app.route('/users/<int:user_id>', methods=['GET'])
def get_user(user_id):
    user = next((user for user in users if user['id'] == user_id), None)
    if user is not None:
        return jsonify(user)
    return jsonify({"error": "User not found"}), 404

@app.route('/users/<int:user_id>', methods=['PUT'])
def update_user(user_id):
    update_data = request.get_json()
    user = next((user for user in users if user['id'] == user_id), None)
    if user is not None:
        user.update(update_data)
        return jsonify(user)
    return jsonify({"error": "User not found"}), 404
```

```
@app.route('/users/<int:user_id>', methods=['DELETE'])
def delete_user(user_id):
    global users
    users = [user for user in users if user['id'] != user_id]
    return '', 204
```

4. Running the Application: To run the application, execute the following command in your terminal:

```bash
python app.py
```

Your API will be accessible at `http://127.0.0.1:5000/`.

Using the Flask API in a Mobile App

For the mobile app, you can use various frameworks like React Native, Flutter, or native development (Java/Kotlin for Android, Swift for iOS). Here's an example using React Native to interact with the Flask API.

1. Setup React Native: First, set up a new React Native project:

```bash
npx react-native init MyApp
cd MyApp
```

2. Install Axios: Axios is a popular HTTP client for making API requests.

```bash
npm install axios
```

3. Making API Calls: In your React Native application, you can use Axios to make API calls to the Flask backend.

```javascript
import React, { useState, useEffect } from 'react';
import { View, Text, Button, FlatList } from 'react-native';
import axios from 'axios';

const App = () => {
```

```jsx
  const [users, setUsers] = useState([]);

  useEffect(() => {
    fetchUsers();
  }, []);

  const fetchUsers = async () => {
    try {
      const response = await axios.get('http://127.0.0.1:5000/users');
      setUsers(response.data);
    } catch (error) {
      console.error(error);
    }
  }
  const addUser = async () => {
    try {
      const newUser = { id: users.length + 1, name: 'New User' };
      await axios.post('http://127.0.0.1:5000/users', newUser);
      fetchUsers();
    } catch (error) {
      console.error(error);
    }
  }
  return (
    <View>
      <Button title="Add User" onPress={addUser} />
```

```
    <FlatList
      data={users}
      keyExtractor={(item) => item.id.toString()}
      renderItem={({ item }) =>
<Text>{item.name}</Text>}
      />
    </View>
  );
  export default App;
  ```

Flask provides a simple yet powerful framework for building APIs that can serve as the backend for mobile applications. Its flexibility, ease of use, and strong community support make it an excellent choice for developers looking to build scalable and maintainable mobile apps. By following the steps outlined above, you can quickly set up a Flask API and integrate it with a mobile app, leveraging the strengths of both technologies to deliver a seamless user experience.

Setting Up Your Flask Development Environment for Mobile App Development

Flask is a micro web framework written in Python that is well-suited for developing web applications, particularly RESTful APIs that can serve as backends for mobile applications. In this guide, we will cover the steps necessary to set up a robust Flask development environment tailored for mobile app development. This setup includes installing Flask, configuring the environment, setting up database connectivity, creating and testing API endpoints, and integrating with a mobile app.

1. Installing Flask

To start, you need to have Python installed on your system. Flask works with Python 3.6 and above. Verify your Python installation by running:

```bash
python --version
```

If Python is installed, you can proceed to create a virtual environment to keep your project dependencies isolated. Use the following commands:

```bash
# Install virtualenv if you don't have it
pip install virtualenv

# Create a virtual environment
```

```
virtualenv venv

# Activate the virtual environment
# On Windows:
venv\Scripts\activate
# On macOS/Linux:
source venv/bin/activate
```

With the virtual environment activated, install Flask:

```bash
pip install Flask
```

2. Setting Up the Project Structure

Create a project directory and navigate into it. Inside this directory, create the following structure:

```
my_flask_app/
   app/
      __init__.py
      routes.py
      models.py
      config.py
```

```
tests/
    test_routes.py
venv/
run.py
```

- `app/`: Contains the application logic.
- `tests/`: Contains unit tests.
- `venv/`: The virtual environment.
- `run.py`: Entry point to run the application.

3. Configuring the Flask Application

In `app/__init__.py`, initialize the Flask application and configure it:

```python
from flask import Flask
from flask_sqlalchemy import SQLAlchemy

db = SQLAlchemy()

def create_app():
    app = Flask(__name__)
```

```
    app.config.from_object('app.config.Config')
    db.init_app(app)

    with app.app_context():
        from . import routes
        db.create_all()
    return app
```

In `app/config.py`, add configuration settings:

```python
import os

class Config:
    SECRET_KEY = os.urandom(24)
    SQLALCHEMY_DATABASE_URI = 'sqlite:///site.db'
    SQLALCHEMY_TRACK_MODIFICATIONS = False
```

4. Setting Up Database Models

In `app/models.py`, define the database models. For example, a simple User model:

```python
from . import db

class User(db.Model):
    id = db.Column(db.Integer, primary_key=True)
    username = db.Column(db.String(20), unique=True, nullable=False)
    email = db.Column(db.String(120), unique=True, nullable=False)
    password = db.Column(db.String(60), nullable=False)

    def __repr__(self):
        return f"User('{self.username}', '{self.email}')"
```

5. Creating API Endpoints

In `app/routes.py`, define the API endpoints:

```python
from flask import jsonify, request, Blueprint
from . import db
from .models import User

bp = Blueprint('main', __name__)

@bp.route('/users', methods=['GET'])
```

```python
def get_users():
    users = User.query.all()
    return jsonify([user.username for user in users])

@bp.route('/users', methods=['POST'])
def add_user():
    data = request.get_json()
    new_user = User(username=data['username'], email=data['email'], password=data['password'])
    db.session.add(new_user)
    db.session.commit()
    return jsonify({'message': 'User created!'}), 201

def init_app(app):
    app.register_blueprint(bp)
```

Update `app/__init__.py` to include the routes:

```python
# ... existing code ...

def create_app():
    # ... existing code ...

    from .routes import init_app
    init_app(app)
```

    return app
```

## 6. Running the Application

Create `run.py` to serve as the entry point for your application:

```python
from app import create_app

app = create_app()

if __name__ == '__main__':
    app.run(debug=True)
```

Run your Flask application:

```bash
python run.py
```

Your API should now be accessible at `http://127.0.0.1:5000/users`.
```

7. Setting Up Unit Tests

Testing is crucial for ensuring the reliability of your API. In `tests/test_routes.py`, add unit tests for your endpoints:

```python
import unittest
from app import create_app, db
from app.models import User

class RoutesTestCase(unittest.TestCase):

    def setUp(self):
        self.app = create_app()
        self.app.config['TESTING'] = True
        self.app.config['SQLALCHEMY_DATABASE_URI'] = 'sqlite:///:memory:'
        self.client = self.app.test_client()
        with self.app.app_context():
            db.create_all()

    def tearDown(self):
        with self.app.app_context():
            db.session.remove()
            db.drop_all()
```

```python
    def test_get_users(self):
        response = self.client.get('/users')
        self.assertEqual(response.status_code, 200)

    def test_add_user(self):
        response = self.client.post('/users', json={
            'username': 'testuser',
            'email': 'test@example.com',
            'password': 'password123'
        })
        self.assertEqual(response.status_code, 201)

if __name__ == '__main__':
    unittest.main()
```

Run the tests with:

```bash
python -m unittest discover -s tests
```

8. Integrating with a Mobile App

To interact with your Flask API from a mobile application, you can use frameworks like React Native,

Flutter, or native development approaches. Here's a simple example using React Native.

1. Setup React Native: Create a new React Native project:

```bash
npx react-native init MyApp
cd MyApp
```

2. Install Axios: Axios is used for making HTTP requests:

```bash
npm install axios
```

3. Making API Calls: In your React Native application, create a component to fetch and display users:

```javascript
import React, { useState, useEffect } from 'react';
import { View, Text, Button, FlatList } from 'react-native';
import axios from 'axios';
```

```
const App = () => {
  const [users, setUsers] = useState([]);

  useEffect(() => {
    fetchUsers();
  }, []);

  const fetchUsers = async () => {
    try {
      const response = await axios.get('http://127.0.0.1:5000/users');
      setUsers(response.data);
    } catch (error) {
      console.error(error);
    }
  }
  const addUser = async () => {
    try {
      const newUser = { username: 'newuser', email: 'newuser@example.com', password: 'password' };
      await axios.post('http://127.0.0.1:5000/users', newUser);
      fetchUsers();
    } catch (error) {
      console.error(error);
    }
  }
  return (
    <View>
```

```
      <Button title="Add User" onPress={addUser} />
      <FlatList
        data={users}
        keyExtractor={(item) => item.id.toString()}
        renderItem={({ item }) =>
<Text>{item.username}</Text>}
      />
    </View>
  );
  export default App;
```
```

Setting up a Flask development environment for mobile app development involves several steps, from installation to creating a robust API and integrating it with a mobile application. Flask's simplicity and flexibility make it an excellent choice for backend development. By following the outlined steps, you can create a scalable and maintainable Flask backend that serves as the foundation for your mobile applications. This environment not only facilitates the development process but also ensures that your application is well-structured, tested, and ready for integration with various mobile platforms.
```

Your First Flask Application - Hello, World!

Flask is a micro web framework for Python, known for its simplicity and flexibility. It is an excellent choice for developers looking to create web applications and RESTful APIs quickly. In this tutorial, we will walk you through the process of creating your first Flask application, a simple "Hello, World!" project, and then extend it to a basic API that can be used in mobile app development.

1. Setting Up Your Environment

Before we start coding, let's set up our development environment. Ensure that Python is installed on your machine. Flask requires Python 3.6 or higher.

First, create a project directory and navigate into it:

```bash
mkdir my_flask_app
cd my_flask_app
```

Next, set up a virtual environment to manage dependencies:

```bash
# Install virtualenv if you don't have it
pip install virtualenv

# Create a virtual environment
virtualenv venv

# Activate the virtual environment
# On Windows:
venv\Scripts\activate
# On macOS/Linux:
source venv/bin/activate
```

With the virtual environment activated, install Flask:

```bash
pip install Flask
```

2. Creating the Flask Application

Create a new file named `app.py` in your project directory. This file will contain the code for your Flask application.

```python
```

```
from flask import Flask

app = Flask(__name__)

@app.route('/')
def hello_world():
    return "Hello, World!"

if __name__ == '__main__':
    app.run(debug=True)
```
```

Let's break down this code:

- **Importing Flask:** The `Flask` class is imported from the `flask` module.

- **Creating an instance of the Flask class:** `app = Flask(__name__)` creates the Flask application instance.

- **Defining a route:** The `@app.route('/')` decorator defines the route for the root URL (`/`). The function `hello_world()` is called when this route is accessed.
```

- **Running the application:**
  `app.run(debug=True)` runs the Flask development server. The `debug=True` parameter enables debug mode, which provides helpful error messages and automatically restarts the server when code changes.

To run your application, execute the following command:

```bash
python app.py
```

Open your web browser and navigate to `http://127.0.0.1:5000/`. You should see the message "Hello, World!".

3. Extending to a Basic API

Now, let's extend this simple application into a basic API that can be used in mobile app development. We'll create an API endpoint to manage user data.

First, we need to create a directory structure to organize our code better:

```
my_flask_app/
  app/
    __init__.py
    routes.py
    models.py
    config.py
  venv/
  run.py
```

- `app/`: Contains the application logic.

- `venv/`: The virtual environment.

- `run.py`: Entry point to run the application.

4. Configuring the Flask Application

In `app/__init__.py`, initialize the Flask application and configure it:

```python
from flask import Flask
from flask_sqlalchemy import SQLAlchemy

db = SQLAlchemy()
```

```
def create_app():
    app = Flask(__name__)
    app.config.from_object('app.config.Config')
    db.init_app(app)

    with app.app_context():
        from . import routes
        db.create_all()
    return app
```

In `app/config.py`, add configuration settings:

```python
import os

class Config:
    SECRET_KEY = os.urandom(24)
    SQLALCHEMY_DATABASE_URI = 'sqlite:///site.db'
    SQLALCHEMY_TRACK_MODIFICATIONS = False
```

5. Setting Up Database Models

In `app/models.py`, define the database models. Here is an example of a simple User model:

```python
from . import db

class User(db.Model):
    id = db.Column(db.Integer, primary_key=True)
    username = db.Column(db.String(20), unique=True, nullable=False)
    email = db.Column(db.String(120), unique=True, nullable=False)
    password = db.Column(db.String(60), nullable=False)

    def __repr__(self):
        return f"User('{self.username}', '{self.email}')"
```

6. Creating API Endpoints

In `app/routes.py`, define the API endpoints:

```python
from flask import jsonify, request, Blueprint
from . import db
from .models import User
```

```python
bp = Blueprint('main', __name__)

@bp.route('/users', methods=['GET'])
def get_users():
    users = User.query.all()
    return jsonify([user.username for user in users])

@bp.route('/users', methods=['POST'])
def add_user():
    data = request.get_json()
    new_user = User(username=data['username'], email=data['email'], password=data['password'])
    db.session.add(new_user)
    db.session.commit()
    return jsonify({'message': 'User created!'}), 201

def init_app(app):
    app.register_blueprint(bp)
```

Update `app/__init__.py` to include the routes:

```python
# ... existing code ...

def create_app():
    # ... existing code ...
```

```
from .routes import init_app
init_app(app)

return app
```

7. Running the Application

Create `run.py` to serve as the entry point for your application:

```python
from app import create_app

app = create_app()

if __name__ == '__main__':
    app.run(debug=True)
```

Run your Flask application:

```bash
python run.py
```

Your API should now be accessible at
`http://127.0.0.1:5000/users`.

8. Testing the API

Testing is an essential part of API development. Here are a few ways to test your endpoints:

- **Using Postman:** Postman is a popular tool for testing APIs. You can send GET and POST requests to your API endpoints to verify they are working correctly.

- **Curl**: You can use curl in the terminal to make requests.

For example, to test the `GET /users` endpoint:

```bash
curl http://127.0.0.1:5000/users
```

To test the `POST /users` endpoint:

```bash
```

```
curl -X POST -H "Content-Type: application/json" -d
'{"username":"testuser", "email":"test@example.com",
"password":"password123"}' http://127.0.0.1:5000/users
```

Congratulations! You have successfully created your first Flask application and extended it to a basic API suitable for mobile app development. Flask's simplicity and flexibility make it an excellent choice for developing backend services. By following the steps outlined in this tutorial, you have set up a Flask development environment, created a "Hello, World!" application, and expanded it to handle user data via API endpoints.

This foundational knowledge provides a stepping stone for more advanced Flask applications and integrations with mobile applications. As you continue to develop with Flask, you can explore more features such as authentication, authorization, and more complex data models to build robust and scalable applications.

Understanding Flask's Core Components (Routes, Views, Templates)

Flask is a micro web framework for Python that is widely used for developing web applications and RESTful APIs. Its simplicity and flexibility make it a favorite among developers. To build effective applications with Flask, it's essential to understand its core components: routes, views, and templates. This article will delve into these components and how they work together to create a functional web application, with a focus on building APIs for mobile app development.

1. Routes

Routes in Flask are used to map URLs to functions. When a user visits a specific URL, Flask knows which function to execute based on the route. This is achieved using the `@app.route` decorator.

Here's a simple example to illustrate how routes work:

```python
from flask import Flask

app = Flask(__name__)

@app.route('/')
def home():
    return "Welcome to the Home Page"

@app.route('/about')
def about():
```

```
    return "About Page"

if __name__ == '__main__':
    app.run(debug=True)
```

In this example:

- The root URL (`/`) is mapped to the `home` function, which returns a welcome message.

- The `/about` URL is mapped to the `about` function, which returns an "About Page" message.

When you run this application and navigate to `http://127.0.0.1:5000/`, you'll see "Welcome to the Home Page". Visiting `http://127.0.0.1:5000/about` will display "About Page".

2. Views

Views in Flask are the functions that handle the logic of what happens when a specific route is accessed. They can return various types of responses, such as HTML, JSON, or even redirect to another route.

For API development, views often return JSON responses. Here's an example of a view returning JSON data:

```python
from flask import Flask, jsonify

app = Flask(__name__)

@app.route('/api/data')
def get_data():
    data = {
        "name": "John Doe",
        "age": 30,
        "city": "New York"
    }
    return jsonify(data)

if __name__ == '__main__':
    app.run(debug=True)
```

In this example:

- The `/api/data` route is mapped to the `get_data` view function.

- The `get_data` function returns a JSON object using Flask's `jsonify` function.

When you run this application and visit `http://127.0.0.1:5000/api/data`, you'll see the JSON data displayed in your browser.

3. Templates

Templates in Flask are used to render HTML content dynamically. Flask uses Jinja2 as its template engine, allowing you to create HTML files with placeholders that are replaced with dynamic data when the template is rendered.

Here's how you can set up templates in Flask:

1. Directory Structure:
```
my_flask_app/
   app.py
   templates/
      index.html
      about.html
```

2. Creating Templates:

- `templates/index.html`:
  ```html
  <!DOCTYPE html>
  <html>
  <head>
      <title>Home Page</title>
  </head>
  <body>
      <h1>{{ message }}</h1>
  </body>
  </html>
  ```

- `templates/about.html`:
  ```html
  <!DOCTYPE html>
  <html>
  <head>
      <title>About Page</title>
  </head>
  <body>
      <h1>About Us</h1>
      <p>{{ description }}</p>
  </body>
  </html>
  ```

3. Using Templates in Views:

```python
from flask import Flask, render_template

app = Flask(__name__)

@app.route('/')
def home():
    return render_template('index.html', message="Welcome to the Home Page")

@app.route('/about')
def about():
    return render_template('about.html', description="This is the about page.")

if __name__ == '__main__':
    app.run(debug=True)
```

In this example:

- The `render_template` function is used to render HTML templates.

- The `home` view renders the `index.html` template and passes a dynamic message to it.

- The `about` view renders the `about.html` template and passes a description to it.

4. Integrating Flask Components for a Mobile App API

Now, let's combine routes, views, and templates to create a basic API for mobile app development.

1. Project Structure:
```
my_flask_app/
    app/
        __init__.py
        routes.py
        models.py
        templates/
            index.html
    run.py
    venv/
```

2. Creating the Application Factory:
- `app/__init__.py`:
```python
from flask import Flask
```

```python
from flask_sqlalchemy import SQLAlchemy

db = SQLAlchemy()

def create_app():
    app = Flask(__name__)

app.config['SQLALCHEMY_DATABASE_URI'] = 'sqlite:///site.db'

app.config['SQLALCHEMY_TRACK_MODIFICATIONS'] = False
    db.init_app(app)

    with app.app_context():
        from . import routes
        db.create_all()
        return app
```

3. Defining Models:
- `app/models.py`:
```python
from . import db

class User(db.Model):
    id = db.Column(db.Integer, primary_key=True)
```

```python
    username = db.Column(db.String(20), unique=True, nullable=False)
    email = db.Column(db.String(120), unique=True, nullable=False)
    password = db.Column(db.String(60), nullable=False)

    def __repr__(self):
        return f"User('{self.username}', '{self.email}')"
```

4. Creating Routes and Views:
- `app/routes.py`:
```python
from flask import render_template, request, jsonify, Blueprint
from . import db
from .models import User

bp = Blueprint('main', __name__)

@bp.route('/')
def home():
    return render_template('index.html', message="Welcome to the Home Page")

@bp.route('/api/users', methods=['GET'])
```

```python
def get_users():
    users = User.query.all()
    return jsonify([user.username for user in users])

@bp.route('/api/users', methods=['POST'])
def add_user():
    data = request.get_json()
    new_user = User(username=data['username'], email=data['email'], password=data['password'])
    db.session.add(new_user)
    db.session.commit()
    return jsonify({'message': 'User created!'}), 201

def init_app(app):
    app.register_blueprint(bp)
```

5. Running the Application:
- `run.py`:
```python
from app import create_app

app = create_app()

if __name__ == '__main__':
    app.run(debug=True)
```

6. Creating a Template:
   - `app/templates/index.html`:
     ```html
     <!DOCTYPE html>
     <html>
     <head>
        <title>Home Page</title>
     </head>
     <body>
        <h1>{{ message }}</h1>
     </body>
     </html>
     ```

Understanding Flask's core components—routes, views, and templates—is crucial for developing robust web applications and APIs. Routes define how URLs map to functions, views handle the logic for each route, and templates dynamically render HTML content. By combining these components, you can create powerful and flexible web applications and APIs, which can serve as the backend for mobile applications.

This foundational knowledge will allow you to build more complex applications, implement additional features, and create scalable solutions. As you continue to work with Flask, you will find it to be an incredibly versatile tool that adapts to your project's needs, whether you're building a simple website or a complex mobile app backend.

Chapter 2

Demystifying RESTful Architecture - Principles and Benefits

RESTful architecture has become a dominant design pattern for web services, particularly in the realm of mobile app development. REST (Representational State Transfer) provides a set of guidelines for creating scalable, maintainable, and interoperable APIs. This article explores the core principles of RESTful architecture, its benefits, and demonstrates how to implement a RESTful API using Flask for mobile app development.

Principles of RESTful Architecture

RESTful architecture is based on a few key principles that ensure the creation of a robust and efficient API:

1. Client-Server Separation:

- The client and server operate independently. The client is responsible for the user interface and user experience, while the server handles data storage and business logic.

- This separation allows each to be developed and scaled independently.

2. Statelessness:

- Each request from a client to the server must contain all the information needed to understand and process the request. The server does not store any client context between requests.

- This principle simplifies the server design and enhances scalability, as the server does not need to maintain any session information.

3. Cacheability:

- Responses must define themselves as cacheable or not to prevent clients from reusing stale or inappropriate data.

- Proper use of caching can reduce the number of interactions between the client and server, improving performance and scalability.

4. Uniform Interface:

- A uniform interface simplifies and decouples the architecture, which enables each part to evolve independently.

- It includes resource identification, resource manipulation through representations, self-descriptive messages, and hypermedia as the engine of application state (HATEOAS).

5. Layered System:

- A client cannot ordinarily tell whether it is connected directly to the end server or an intermediary along the way. This structure allows for load balancing, security layers, and shared caches.

6. Code on Demand (optional):

- Servers can extend client functionality by transferring executable code. For example, delivering JavaScript to a web client.

Benefits of RESTful Architecture

Adopting RESTful architecture for your APIs provides numerous benefits:

1. Scalability: Statelessness and client-server separation enable easy scaling of the server components. Multiple servers can handle requests without sharing any client state.

2. Performance: Caching can significantly improve the performance of the system by reducing the server load and decreasing response times.

3. Flexibility and Modularity: A uniform interface and the separation of concerns allow each component of the application to be developed and maintained independently.

4. Interoperability: RESTful APIs use standard HTTP methods and can be consumed by any client that understands HTTP, making them highly interoperable.

5. Simplicity: The use of standard methods and statelessness makes the APIs easier to understand and implement.

Implementing a RESTful API with Flask

To illustrate these principles, let's create a simple RESTful API using Flask for a mobile app backend.

1. Setup and Configuration

First, ensure you have Python and Flask installed. Create a project directory and set up a virtual environment:

```bash
mkdir my_restful_api
cd my_restful_api
python -m venv venv
source venv/bin/activate
pip install Flask
```

2. Project Structure

Organize your project as follows:

```
my_restful_api/
   app/
      __init__.py
      models.py
      routes.py
      config.py
   run.py
   venv/
```

```

## 3. Creating the Flask Application

Initialize the Flask application and configure it in `app/__init__.py`:

```python
from flask import Flask
from flask_sqlalchemy import SQLAlchemy

db = SQLAlchemy()

def create_app():
    app = Flask(__name__)
    app.config.from_object('app.config.Config')
    db.init_app(app)

    with app.app_context():
        from . import routes
        db.create_all()
        return app
```

Define the configuration in `app/config.py`:

```python

```
import os

class Config:
    SECRET_KEY = os.urandom(24)
    SQLALCHEMY_DATABASE_URI = 'sqlite:///site.db'
    SQLALCHEMY_TRACK_MODIFICATIONS = False
```

4. Defining Models

Define a simple User model in `app/models.py`:

```python
from . import db

class User(db.Model):
    id = db.Column(db.Integer, primary_key=True)
    username = db.Column(db.String(20), unique=True, nullable=False)
    email = db.Column(db.String(120), unique=True, nullable=False)
    password = db.Column(db.String(60), nullable=False)

    def __repr__(self):
        return f"User('{self.username}', '{self.email}')"
```

```

## 5. Creating Routes

Define the API routes in `app/routes.py`:

```python
from flask import Blueprint, request, jsonify
from . import db
from .models import User

bp = Blueprint('api', __name__)

@bp.route('/users', methods=['GET'])
def get_users():
    users = User.query.all()
    return jsonify([user.username for user in users])

@bp.route('/users', methods=['POST'])
def create_user():
    data = request.get_json()
    new_user = User(username=data['username'], email=data['email'], password=data['password'])
    db.session.add(new_user)
    db.session.commit()
    return jsonify({'message': 'User created!'}), 201

```python
@bp.route('/users/<int:id>', methods=['GET'])
def get_user(id):
    user = User.query.get_or_404(id)
    return jsonify({'username': user.username, 'email': user.email})

@bp.route('/users/<int:id>', methods=['PUT'])
def update_user(id):
    data = request.get_json()
    user = User.query.get_or_404(id)
    user.username = data['username']
    user.email = data['email']
    user.password = data['password']
    db.session.commit()
    return jsonify({'message': 'User updated!'})

@bp.route('/users/<int:id>', methods=['DELETE'])
def delete_user(id):
    user = User.query.get_or_404(id)
    db.session.delete(user)
    db.session.commit()
    return jsonify({'message': 'User deleted!'})

def init_app(app):
    app.register_blueprint(bp, url_prefix='/api')
```
```
```

6. Running the Application

Create an entry point to run the application in `run.py`:

```python
from app import create_app

app = create_app()

if __name__ == '__main__':
    app.run(debug=True)
```

Run the application:

```bash
python run.py
```

Your API will be accessible at `http://127.0.0.1:5000/api/users`.

Testing the API

You can test the API using tools like Postman or curl:

Get all users:

```bash
curl http://127.0.0.1:5000/api/users
```

Create a new user:

```bash
curl -X POST -H "Content-Type: application/json" -d '{"username":"john", "email":"john@example.com", "password":"password"}' http://127.0.0.1:5000/api/users
```

Get a specific user:

```bash
curl http://127.0.0.1:5000/api/users/1
```

Update a user:

```bash
curl -X PUT -H "Content-Type: application/json" -d '{"username":"john_updated", "email":"john_updated@example.com", "password":"newpassword"}' http://127.0.0.1:5000/api/users/1
```

```

### Delete a user:
```bash
curl -X DELETE http://127.0.0.1:5000/api/users/1
```

Understanding and implementing RESTful architecture is crucial for developing scalable and maintainable APIs, especially for mobile app development. The principles of REST—client-server separation, statelessness, cacheability, uniform interface, layered system, and optional code on demand—provide a solid foundation for building robust APIs.

By following these principles and leveraging Flask, you can create powerful APIs that are easy to develop, test, and scale. The example provided demonstrates a simple yet effective approach to implementing a RESTful API using Flask, showcasing how these principles translate into practical application.

As you continue to develop RESTful APIs, you will find that adhering to these principles not only improves the performance and scalability of your applications but also enhances their maintainability and flexibility, making it easier to evolve and adapt to changing requirements.
```

Designing Powerful RESTful Endpoints for Your Mobile App

Designing powerful RESTful endpoints is crucial for creating efficient and maintainable APIs that serve as the backbone of mobile applications. RESTful architecture, with its principles of statelessness, client-server separation, and a uniform interface, offers a robust framework for building these APIs. In this article, we'll explore how to design RESTful endpoints using Flask, a popular Python microframework, to support a mobile app.

Key Principles of RESTful API Design

1. Resource Identification: Resources should be identified using URIs (Uniform Resource Identifiers). For instance, `/users` for a collection of user resources and `/users/{id}` for a specific user.

2. HTTP Methods: Use standard HTTP methods (GET, POST, PUT, DELETE, PATCH) to perform CRUD operations on resources:

- `GET`: Retrieve data.

- `POST`: Create a new resource.

- `PUT`: Update an existing resource.

- `DELETE`: Delete a resource.

- `PATCH`: Partially update a resource.

3. Statelessness: Each request from a client to the server must contain all the information needed to understand and process the request. The server does not store any client context between requests.

4. Data Representation: Use standard formats like JSON or XML for data interchange. JSON is the most common format due to its simplicity and wide adoption.

5. Error Handling: Return appropriate HTTP status codes and messages for errors (e.g., 404 for not found, 400 for bad request, 500 for server error).

6. Versioning: Implement versioning for your API to ensure backward compatibility (e.g., `/v1/users`).

Setting Up Flask for RESTful API

Let's start by setting up a Flask project. Create a project directory and set up a virtual environment:

```bash
mkdir my_restful_api
cd my_restful_api
python -m venv venv
source venv/bin/activate
pip install Flask
```

1. Project Structure:

```
my_restful_api/
    app/
        __init__.py
        models.py
        routes.py
        config.py
    run.py
    venv/
```

2. Creating the Flask Application:

Initialize the Flask application and configure it in `app/__init__.py`:

```python
```

```python
from flask import Flask
from flask_sqlalchemy import SQLAlchemy

db = SQLAlchemy()

def create_app():
    app = Flask(__name__)
    app.config.from_object('app.config.Config')
    db.init_app(app)

    with app.app_context():
        from . import routes
        db.create_all()
        return app
```

Define the configuration in `app/config.py`:

```python
import os

class Config:
    SECRET_KEY = os.urandom(24)
    SQLALCHEMY_DATABASE_URI = 'sqlite:///site.db'
    SQLALCHEMY_TRACK_MODIFICATIONS = False
```

```

### 3. Defining Models:

Define a simple User model in `app/models.py`:

```python
from . import db

class User(db.Model):
    id = db.Column(db.Integer, primary_key=True)
    username = db.Column(db.String(20), unique=True, nullable=False)
    email = db.Column(db.String(120), unique=True, nullable=False)
    password = db.Column(db.String(60), nullable=False)

    def __repr__(self):
        return f"User('{self.username}', '{self.email}')"
```

4. Creating Routes and Views:

Define the API routes in `app/routes.py`:

```python
from flask import Blueprint, request, jsonify
```
```

```python
from . import db
from .models import User

bp = Blueprint('api', __name__)

@bp.route('/users', methods=['GET'])
def get_users():
    users = User.query.all()
    return jsonify([user.to_dict() for user in users])

@bp.route('/users', methods=['POST'])
def create_user():
    data = request.get_json()
    new_user = User(username=data['username'], email=data['email'], password=data['password'])
    db.session.add(new_user)
    db.session.commit()
    return jsonify(new_user.to_dict()), 201

@bp.route('/users/<int:id>', methods=['GET'])
def get_user(id):
    user = User.query.get_or_404(id)
    return jsonify(user.to_dict())

@bp.route('/users/<int:id>', methods=['PUT'])
def update_user(id):
    data = request.get_json()
```

```python
    user = User.query.get_or_404(id)
    user.username = data['username']
    user.email = data['email']
    user.password = data['password']
    db.session.commit()
    return jsonify(user.to_dict())

@bp.route('/users/<int:id>', methods=['DELETE'])
def delete_user(id):
    user = User.query.get_or_404(id)
    db.session.delete(user)
    db.session.commit()
    return jsonify({'message': 'User deleted!'})

def init_app(app):
    app.register_blueprint(bp, url_prefix='/api')
```

To make the User model serializable to JSON, add a `to_dict` method in `app/models.py`:

```python
class User(db.Model):
    # ... existing fields ...

    def to_dict(self):
        return {
```

```
            'id': self.id,
            'username': self.username,
            'email': self.email
        }
```

5. Running the Application:

Create an entry point to run the application in `run.py`:

```python
from app import create_app

app = create_app()

if __name__ == '__main__':
    app.run(debug=True)
```

Run the application:

```bash
python run.py
```

Your API will be accessible at `http://127.0.0.1:5000/api/users`.

Designing Powerful RESTful Endpoints

Now that we have a basic setup, let's delve into designing powerful RESTful endpoints.

1. Handling Complex Queries:

Allow clients to filter, sort, and paginate data. This makes the API more flexible and reduces the need for multiple endpoints.

```python
@bp.route('/users', methods=['GET'])
def get_users():
    username = request.args.get('username')
    email = request.args.get('email')
    query = User.query

    if username:
        query = query.filter_by(username=username)
    if email:
        query = query.filter_by(email=email)

    page = request.args.get('page', 1, type=int)
    per_page = request.args.get('per_page', 10, type=int)
    users = query.paginate(page, per_page, False).items
```

```
    return jsonify([user.to_dict() for user in users])
```

2. Implementing Authentication:

Secure your endpoints by implementing authentication, such as token-based authentication.

First, install Flask-JWT-Extended:

```bash
pip install Flask-JWT-Extended
```

Update `app/__init__.py` to include JWT:

```python
from flask_jwt_extended import JWTManager

def create_app():
    app = Flask(__name__)
    app.config.from_object('app.config.Config')
    db.init_app(app)
    jwt = JWTManager(app)

    with app.app_context():
```

```
    from . import routes
    db.create_all()
    return app
```

Update `app/config.py` with a JWT secret key:

```python
class Config:
    SECRET_KEY = os.urandom(24)
    SQLALCHEMY_DATABASE_URI = 'sqlite:///site.db'
    SQLALCHEMY_TRACK_MODIFICATIONS = False
    JWT_SECRET_KEY = 'your_jwt_secret_key'
```

Add login and protected routes in `app/routes.py`:

```python
from flask_jwt_extended import create_access_token, jwt_required, get_jwt_identity

@bp.route('/login', methods=['POST'])
def login():
    data = request.get_json()
```

```
    user = User.query.filter_by(username=data['username']).first()
    if user and user.password == data['password']:
        access_token = create_access_token(identity=user.id)
        return jsonify(access_token=access_token)
    return jsonify({"msg": "Bad username or password"}), 401

@bp.route('/protected', methods=['GET'])
@jwt_required()
def protected():
    current_user_id = get_jwt_identity()
    user = User.query.get_or_404(current_user_id)
    return jsonify(user.to_dict())
```

3. Error Handling:

Implement proper error handling to provide meaningful error messages to clients.

```python
@app.errorhandler(404)
def resource_not_found(e):
    return jsonify(error=str(e)), 404
```

```python
@app.errorhandler(400)
def bad_request(e):
    return jsonify(error=str(e)), 400

@app.errorhandler(500)
def internal_server_error(e):
    return jsonify(error=str(e)), 500
```

4. API Versioning:

Support multiple versions of your API to ensure backward compatibility.

Update `app/routes.py` to include versioning:

```python
bp_v1 = Blueprint('api_v1', __name__)

@bp_v1.route('/users', methods=['GET'])
def get_users_v1():
    # V1 logic here
    pass

@bp_v1.route('/users', methods=['POST'])
def create_user_v1():
    # V1 logic here
```

```
    pass

bp_v2 = Blueprint('api_v2', __name__)

@bp_v2.route('/users', methods=['GET'])
def get_users_v2():
    # V2 logic here
    pass

@bp_v2.route('/users', methods=['POST'])
def create_user_v2():
    # V2 logic here
    pass

def init_app(app):
    app.register_blue
```

```python
from flask import Flask
from flask_sqlalchemy import SQLAlchemy
from flask_jwt_extended import JWTManager

db = SQLAlchemy()

def create_app():
    app = Flask(__name__)
    app.config.from_object('app.config.Config')
```

```
    db.init_app(app)
    jwt = JWTManager(app)

    with app.app_context():
        from . import routes
        db.create_all()
        routes.init_app(app)
        return app
```

In `app/routes.py`, define the blueprints for different versions:

```python
from flask import Blueprint, request, jsonify
from . import db
from .models import User
from flask_jwt_extended import create_access_token, jwt_required, get_jwt_identity

bp_v1 = Blueprint('api_v1', __name__)
bp_v2 = Blueprint('api_v2', __name__)

# V1 endpoints
@bp_v1.route('/users', methods=['GET'])
def get_users_v1():
    users = User.query.all()
```

```python
    return jsonify([user.to_dict() for user in users])

@bp_v1.route('/users', methods=['POST'])
def create_user_v1():
    data = request.get_json()
    new_user = User(username=data['username'], email=data['email'], password=data['password'])
    db.session.add(new_user)
    db.session.commit()
    return jsonify(new_user.to_dict()), 201

# V2 endpoints with enhanced functionality (e.g., better error handling)
@bp_v2.route('/users', methods=['GET'])
def get_users_v2():
    username = request.args.get('username')
    email = request.args.get('email')
    query = User.query

    if username:
        query = query.filter_by(username=username)
    if email:
        query = query.filter_by(email=email)

    page = request.args.get('page', 1, type=int)
    per_page = request.args.get('per_page', 10, type=int)
    users = query.paginate(page, per_page, False).items
```

```python
    return jsonify([user.to_dict() for user in users])

@bp_v2.route('/users', methods=['POST'])
def create_user_v2():
    data = request.get_json()
    if 'username' not in data or 'email' not in data or 'password' not in data:
        return jsonify({"error": "Missing required parameters"}), 400
    new_user = User(username=data['username'], email=data['email'], password=data['password'])
    db.session.add(new_user)
    db.session.commit()
    return jsonify(new_user.to_dict()), 201

# Authentication and protected routes
@bp_v1.route('/login', methods=['POST'])
@bp_v2.route('/login', methods=['POST'])
def login():
    data = request.get_json()
    user = User.query.filter_by(username=data['username']).first()
    if user and user.password == data['password']:
        access_token = create_access_token(identity=user.id)
        return jsonify(access_token=access_token)
```

```
    return jsonify({"msg": "Bad username or password"}),
401

@bp_v1.route('/protected', methods=['GET'])
@bp_v2.route('/protected', methods=['GET'])
@jwt_required()
def protected():
    current_user_id = get_jwt_identity()
    user = User.query.get_or_404(current_user_id)
    return jsonify(user.to_dict())

def init_app(app):
    app.register_blueprint(bp_v1, url_prefix='/api/v1')
    app.register_blueprint(bp_v2, url_prefix='/api/v2')
```

Implementing Advanced Features

1. Rate Limiting:

Rate limiting helps to protect your API from abuse by limiting the number of requests a client can make in a given timeframe. Use Flask-Limiter to implement rate limiting:

First, install Flask-Limiter:

```bash
pip install Flask-Limiter
```

Then, integrate it into your application in `app/__init__.py`:

```python
from flask_limiter import Limiter
from flask_limiter.util import get_remote_address

def create_app():
    app = Flask(__name__)
    app.config.from_object('app.config.Config')
    db.init_app(app)
    jwt = JWTManager(app)
    limiter = Limiter(app, key_func=get_remote_address)

    with app.app_context():
        from . import routes
        db.create_all()
        routes.init_app(app)
        return app
```

Apply rate limiting to your routes in `app/routes.py`:

```python
from flask_limiter import Limiter
from flask_limiter.util import get_remote_address

limiter = Limiter(key_func=get_remote_address)

@bp_v2.route('/users', methods=['GET'])
@limiter.limit("10 per minute")
def get_users_v2():
    # Your existing code
    pass

@bp_v2.route('/users', methods=['POST'])
@limiter.limit("5 per minute")
def create_user_v2():
    # Your existing code
    pass
```

2. Documentation:

Good documentation helps developers understand and use your API effectively. Use Flask-RESTPlus for creating self-documenting RESTful APIs:

First, install Flask-RESTPlus:

```bash
pip install Flask-RESTPlus
```

Update your application to include Flask-RESTPlus in `app/__init__.py`:

```python
from flask_restplus import Api

api = Api()

def create_app():
    app = Flask(__name__)
    app.config.from_object('app.config.Config')
    db.init_app(app)
    jwt = JWTManager(app)
    limiter = Limiter(app, key_func=get_remote_address)
    api.init_app(app)

    with app.app_context():
        from . import routes
        db.create_all()
        routes.init_app(app)
        return app
```

Update `app/routes.py` to include API documentation:

```python
from flask_restplus import Namespace, Resource, fields

ns = Namespace('users', description='User operations')

user_model = ns.model('User', {
    'id': fields.Integer(readOnly=True, description='The user unique identifier'),
    'username': fields.String(required=True, description='The username'),
    'email': fields.String(required=True, description='The email address'),
    'password': fields.String(required=True, description='The password')
})

@ns.route('/')
class UserList(Resource):
    @ns.doc('list_users')
    @ns.marshal_list_with(user_model)
    def get(self):
        '''List all users'''
        users = User.query.all()
        return users
```

```python
    @ns.doc('create_user')
    @ns.expect(user_model)
    @ns.marshal_with(user_model, code=201)
    def post(self):
        '''Create a new user'''
        data = ns.payload
        new_user = User(username=data['username'], email=data['email'], password=data['password'])
        db.session.add(new_user)
        db.session.commit()
        return new_user, 201

@ns.route('/<int:id>')
@ns.response(404, 'User not found')
@ns.param('id', 'The user identifier')
class User(Resource):
    @ns.doc('get_user')
    @ns.marshal_with(user_model)
    def get(self, id):
        '''Fetch a user given its identifier'''
        user = User.query.get_or_404(id)
        return user

    @ns.doc('delete_user')
    @ns.response(204, 'User deleted')
    def delete(self, id):
        '''Delete a user given its identifier'''
```

```
        user = User.query.get_or_404(id)
        db.session.delete(user)
        db.session.commit()
        return '', 204

    @ns.expect(user_model)
    @ns.marshal_with(user_model)
    def put(self, id):
        '''Update a user given its identifier'''
        data = ns.payload
        user = User.query.get_or_404(id)
        user.username = data['username']
        user.email = data['email']
        user.password = data['password']
        db.session.commit()
        return user

def init_app(app):
    app.register_blueprint(bp_v1, url_prefix='/api/v1')
    app.register_blueprint(bp_v2, url_prefix='/api/v2')
    api.add_namespace(ns, path='/api/v2/users')
```

1. Testing the API:

First, install Flask-Testing if you haven't already:

```bash
pip install Flask-Testing
```

Create a test file `test_app.py`:

```python
import unittest
from app import create_app, db
from app.models import User

class UserTestCase(unittest.TestCase):

    def setUp(self):
        self.app = create_app()
        self.app.config['TESTING'] = True

self.app.config['SQLALCHEMY_DATABASE_URI'] = 'sqlite:///:memory:'
        self.client = self.app.test_client()
        with self.app.app_context():
            db.create_all()

    def tearDown(self):
        with self.app.app_context():
            db.session.remove()
            db.drop_all()
```

```python
def test_create_user(self):
    response = self.client.post('/api/v2/users', json={
        'username': 'john',
        'email': 'john@example.com',
        'password': 'password'
    })
    self.assertEqual(response.status_code, 201)
    data = response.get_json()
    self.assertEqual(data['username'], 'john')

def test_get_user(self):
    with self.app.app_context():
        user = User(username='john', email='john@example.com', password='password')
        db.session.add(user)
        db.session.commit()

    response = self.client.get(f'/api/v2/users/{user.id}')
    self.assertEqual(response.status_code, 200)
    data = response.get_json()
    self.assertEqual(data['username'], 'john')

def test_update_user(self):
    with self.app.app_context():
        user = User(username='john', email='john@example.com', password='password')
```

```python
        db.session.add(user)
        db.session.commit()

    response = self.client.put(f'/api/v2/users/{user.id}', json={
        'username': 'johnny',
        'email': 'johnny@example.com',
        'password': 'newpassword'
    })
    self.assertEqual(response.status_code, 200)
    data = response.get_json()
    self.assertEqual(data['username'], 'johnny')

def test_delete_user(self):
    with self.app.app_context():
        user = User(username='john', email='john@example.com', password='password')
        db.session.add(user)
        db.session.commit()

    response = self.client.delete(f'/api/v2/users/{user.id}')
    self.assertEqual(response.status_code, 204)

    # Ensure the user is deleted
    response = self.client.get(f'/api/v2/users/{user.id}')
    self.assertEqual(response.status_code, 404)
```

```
if __name__ == '__main__':
    unittest.main()
```

2. Running the Tests:

To run the tests, simply execute the test file:

```bash
python test_app.py
```

Advanced Features and Best Practices

1. Response Caching:

To improve the performance of your API, use caching mechanisms. Flask-Caching can be used to cache responses.

First, install Flask-Caching:

```bash
pip install Flask-Caching
```

Then, configure caching in your application in `app/__init__.py`:

```python
from flask_caching import Cache

def create_app():
    app = Flask(__name__)
    app.config.from_object('app.config.Config')
    db.init_app(app)
    jwt = JWTManager(app)
    limiter = Limiter(app, key_func=get_remote_address)
    cache = Cache(app, config={'CACHE_TYPE': 'simple'})

    with app.app_context():
        from . import routes
        db.create_all()
        routes.init_app(app)
        return app
```

Apply caching to your routes in `app/routes.py`:

```python
from flask_caching import Cache
```

```
cache = Cache()

@bp_v2.route('/users', methods=['GET'])
@cache.cached(timeout=60)
def get_users_v2():
    # Your existing code
    pass
```

2. HATEOAS (Hypermedia as the Engine of Application State):

To make your API more RESTful, include links in your responses to guide the client on available actions. This is part of the HATEOAS constraint.

Modify the `to_dict` method in `app/models.py` to include links:

```python
class User(db.Model):
    # ... existing fields ...

    def to_dict(self):
        return {
            'id': self.id,
            'username': self.username,
```

```
    'email': self.email,
    '_links': {
      'self': f'/api/v2/users/{self.id}',
      'update': f'/api/v2/users/{self.id}',
      'delete': f'/api/v2/users/{self.id}'
    }
```

Designing powerful RESTful endpoints for your mobile app using Flask involves understanding and implementing core REST principles such as statelessness, resource identification, and proper use of HTTP methods. Enhancing your API with advanced features like rate limiting, caching, and HATEOAS ensures your API is robust, performant, and user-friendly.

By following best practices and leveraging Flask's capabilities, you can create a scalable and maintainable backend that supports your mobile app's needs. As the mobile app grows, you can continue to iterate on the API, adding new features, optimizing performance, and maintaining security to provide the best possible experience for your users.

Handling HTTP Methods (GET, POST, PUT, DELETE) in Flask for Mobile App Development

Flask is a micro web framework written in Python, known for its simplicity and flexibility. It is widely used for creating web applications and APIs. In mobile app development, APIs are crucial as they serve as the bridge between the mobile client and the server, allowing data to be exchanged seamlessly. Flask, with its robust support for various HTTP methods, makes it an ideal choice for building RESTful APIs.

HTTP Methods Overview

HTTP methods are fundamental to RESTful APIs. They define the action to be performed for a given resource:

1. GET: Retrieve data from the server.

2. POST: Send data to the server to create a new resource.

3. PUT: Update an existing resource on the server.

4. DELETE: Remove a resource from the server.

Let's explore how to handle these HTTP methods in Flask with practical code examples suitable for a mobile app backend.

Setting Up Flask

First, let's start by setting up a basic Flask application. If you haven't installed Flask yet, you can do so using pip:

```bash
pip install flask
```

Next, create a new file, `app.py`, and set up your Flask application:

```python
from flask import Flask, request, jsonify

app = Flask(__name__)

@app.route('/')
def home():
    return "Welcome to the Flask API!"

if __name__ == '__main__':
    app.run(debug=True)
```

```

This sets up a basic Flask server that you can run with `python app.py`. Now, let's delve into handling each HTTP method.

### Handling GET Requests

GET requests are used to retrieve data from the server. In a mobile app, this could mean fetching user information, posts, or any other data. Here's an example of handling a GET request to retrieve a list of users:

```python
@app.route('/users', methods=['GET'])
def get_users():
    users = [
        {'id': 1, 'name': 'Alice'},
        {'id': 2, 'name': 'Bob'},
        {'id': 3, 'name': 'Charlie'}
    ]
    return jsonify(users)
```

In this example, the `/users` endpoint returns a JSON list of users. The `jsonify` function converts Python
```

dictionaries into JSON responses, which are easily consumable by mobile apps.

Handling POST Requests

POST requests are used to send data to the server to create a new resource. For instance, a mobile app might allow users to register or add new posts. Here's an example of handling a POST request to add a new user:

```python
@app.route('/users', methods=['POST'])
def create_user():
    new_user = request.get_json()
    if 'name' not in new_user:
        return jsonify({'error': 'Name is required'}), 400

    new_user['id'] = 4  # In a real app, you'd generate a unique ID
    return jsonify(new_user), 201
```

In this example, the `/users` endpoint accepts a JSON payload with user details. The `request.get_json()` method parses the incoming JSON request data. We then add a new user (in a real application, this would involve saving the user to a database) and return the created user with a 201 status code, indicating successful creation.

Handling PUT Requests

PUT requests are used to update an existing resource on the server. For instance, a mobile app might allow users to update their profile information. Here's an example of handling a PUT request to update a user's information:

```python
@app.route('/users/<int:user_id>', methods=['PUT'])
def update_user(user_id):
    users = [
        {'id': 1, 'name': 'Alice'},
        {'id': 2, 'name': 'Bob'},
        {'id': 3, 'name': 'Charlie'}
    ]
    user = next((user for user in users if user['id'] == user_id), None)
    if user is None:
        return jsonify({'error': 'User not found'}), 404

    updated_data = request.get_json()
    user.update(updated_data)
    return jsonify(user)
```

In this example, the `/users/<int:user_id>` endpoint accepts a user ID as a URL parameter. We find the user in our list and update their information with the data from the request. The `next` function with a generator expression helps find the user efficiently.

Handling DELETE Requests

DELETE requests are used to remove a resource from the server. For instance, a mobile app might allow users to delete their accounts. Here's an example of handling a DELETE request to remove a user:

```python
@app.route('/users/<int:user_id>', methods=['DELETE'])
def delete_user(user_id):
    users = [
        {'id': 1, 'name': 'Alice'},
        {'id': 2, 'name': 'Bob'},
        {'id': 3, 'name': 'Charlie'}
    ]
    user = next((user for user in users if user['id'] == user_id), None)
    if user is None:
        return jsonify({'error': 'User not found'}), 404
```

```
    users.remove(user)
    return jsonify({'message': 'User deleted successfully'})
```

In this example, the `/users/<int:user_id>` endpoint removes a user with the specified ID from our list. We first check if the user exists and, if so, remove them and return a success message.

Putting It All Together

Here's the complete code for handling all four HTTP methods in a simple Flask application:

```python
from flask import Flask, request, jsonify

app = Flask(__name__)

users = [
    {'id': 1, 'name': 'Alice'},
    {'id': 2, 'name': 'Bob'},
    {'id': 3, 'name': 'Charlie'}
]

@app.route('/users', methods=['GET'])
```

```python
def get_users():
    return jsonify(users)

@app.route('/users', methods=['POST'])
def create_user():
    new_user = request.get_json()
    if 'name' not in new_user:
        return jsonify({'error': 'Name is required'}), 400

    new_user['id'] = max(user['id'] for user in users) + 1
    users.append(new_user)
    return jsonify(new_user), 201

@app.route('/users/<int:user_id>', methods=['PUT'])
def update_user(user_id):
    user = next((user for user in users if user['id'] == user_id), None)
    if user is None:
        return jsonify({'error': 'User not found'}), 404

    updated_data = request.get_json()
    user.update(updated_data)
    return jsonify(user)

@app.route('/users/<int:user_id>', methods=['DELETE'])
def delete_user(user_id):
```

```
    user = next((user for user in users if user['id'] ==
user_id), None)
    if user is None:
        return jsonify({'error': 'User not found'}), 404

    users.remove(user)
    return jsonify({'message': 'User deleted successfully'})

if __name__ == '__main__':
    app.run(debug=True)
```

This code demonstrates a simple but comprehensive API for managing users, including creating, retrieving, updating, and deleting user records.

Testing Your API

You can test your API using tools like Postman or curl. For instance, to test the GET endpoint, you can use the following curl command:

```bash
curl http://127.0.0.1:5000/users
```

To test the POST endpoint, you can use:

```bash
curl -X POST -H "Content-Type: application/json" -d '{"name": "Dave"}' http://127.0.0.1:5000/users
```

For the PUT endpoint:

```bash
curl -X PUT -H "Content-Type: application/json" -d '{"name": "David"}' http://127.0.0.1:5000/users/4
```

And for the DELETE endpoint:

```bash
curl -X DELETE http://127.0.0.1:5000/users/4
```

Handling HTTP methods in Flask is straightforward and flexible, making it an excellent choice for developing APIs for mobile applications. By understanding and implementing GET, POST, PUT, and DELETE methods, you can create robust and efficient APIs that meet the needs of your mobile app users. Flask's simplicity and power allow for rapid development and easy maintenance, ensuring a smooth experience for both developers and users.

Building a Clean API Structure with Blueprints in Flask for Mobile App Development

Flask is a micro web framework that provides a solid foundation for creating web applications and APIs. One of the key features of Flask that enhances modularity and maintainability is Blueprints. Blueprints allow you to organize your application into distinct components, making it easier to manage large applications. This is particularly useful in mobile app development, where a well-structured API can significantly simplify both development and maintenance.

In this article, we'll explore how to build a clean API structure using Blueprints in Flask, complete with code examples.

What are Blueprints?

Blueprints in Flask are essentially components or modules of your application. They allow you to define routes, handlers, and other application features in separate modules, which can then be registered with the main Flask application. This modular approach helps keep the codebase clean and manageable, especially as your application grows.

Setting Up the Project

To get started, let's set up a basic Flask project. First, create a virtual environment and install Flask:

```bash
python3 -m venv venv
source venv/bin/activate
pip install flask
```

Next, create the project directory structure:

```
flask_api/
│
├── app/
│   ├── __init__.py
│   ├── main/
│   │   ├── __init__.py
│   │   ├── routes.py
│   ├── users/
│   │   ├── __init__.py
```

```
|   |   ├── routes.py
|   ├── config.py
├── run.py
```

Initializing the Flask App

In the `app/__init__.py` file, initialize the Flask application and register the Blueprints:

```python
from flask import Flask
from app.main.routes import main
from app.users.routes import users

def create_app():
    app = Flask(__name__)

    # Register Blueprints
    app.register_blueprint(main)
    app.register_blueprint(users)

    return app
```

Creating the Main Blueprint

Create the `main` Blueprint in `app/main/routes.py`:

```python
from flask import Blueprint, jsonify

main = Blueprint('main', __name__)

@main.route('/')
def home():
    return jsonify({"message": "Welcome to the Flask API!"})
```

In this example, the `main` Blueprint handles the home route, returning a simple JSON message.

Creating the Users Blueprint

Create the `users` Blueprint in `app/users/routes.py`:

```python
from flask import Blueprint, request, jsonify

users = Blueprint('users', __name__)

# In-memory data store for users
users_data = [
```

```python
    {'id': 1, 'name': 'Alice'},
    {'id': 2, 'name': 'Bob'},
    {'id': 3, 'name': 'Charlie'}
]

@users.route('/users', methods=['GET'])
def get_users():
    return jsonify(users_data)

@users.route('/users', methods=['POST'])
def create_user():
    new_user = request.get_json()
    if 'name' not in new_user:
        return jsonify({'error': 'Name is required'}), 400

    new_user['id'] = max(user['id'] for user in users_data) + 1
    users_data.append(new_user)
    return jsonify(new_user), 201

@users.route('/users/<int:user_id>', methods=['PUT'])
def update_user(user_id):
    user = next((user for user in users_data if user['id'] == user_id), None)
    if user is None:
        return jsonify({'error': 'User not found'}), 404
```

```
    updated_data = request.get_json()
    user.update(updated_data)
    return jsonify(user)

@users.route('/users/<int:user_id>',
methods=['DELETE'])
def delete_user(user_id):
    user = next((user for user in users_data if user['id'] == user_id), None)
    if user is None:
        return jsonify({'error': 'User not found'}), 404

    users_data.remove(user)
    return jsonify({'message': 'User deleted successfully'})
```

In this example, the `users` Blueprint handles CRUD operations for user resources. We define routes for retrieving, creating, updating, and deleting users.

Configuring the Application

In `app/config.py`, you can define configuration settings for your Flask app. For simplicity, let's leave it empty for now, but this is where you would configure settings such as the database URL, secret keys, etc.

Running the Application

Create the `run.py` file to run the application:

```python
from app import create_app

app = create_app()

if __name__ == '__main__':
    app.run(debug=True)
```

Now, you can run your Flask application with:

```bash
python run.py
```

Testing the API

To test the API, you can use tools like Postman or curl. Here are some examples using curl:

Get all users:

```bash
```

```
curl http://127.0.0.1:5000/users
```

Create a new user:

```bash
curl -X POST -H "Content-Type: application/json" -d '{"name": "Dave"}' http://127.0.0.1:5000/users
```

Update a user:

```bash
curl -X PUT -H "Content-Type: application/json" -d '{"name": "David"}' http://127.0.0.1:5000/users/4
```

Delete a user:

```bash
curl -X DELETE http://127.0.0.1:5000/users/4
```

Adding More Blueprints

As your application grows, you can add more Blueprints to handle different functionalities. For example, you might add a Blueprint for handling authentication, another for managing posts, and so on. Each Blueprint should be defined in its own module, with its routes and views encapsulated within that module.

Example: Adding an Authentication Blueprint

1. Create the `auth` directory and files:

```
app/
├── auth/
│   ├── __init__.py
│   ├── routes.py
```

2. Define the `auth` Blueprint in `app/auth/routes.py`:

```python
from flask import Blueprint, request, jsonify

auth = Blueprint('auth', __name__)

@auth.route('/login', methods=['POST'])
def login():
    data = request.get_json()
```

```
    if data['username'] == 'admin' and data['password'] == 'secret':
        return jsonify({'message': 'Login successful'}), 200
    else:
        return jsonify({'message': 'Invalid credentials'}), 401
```

3. Register the `auth` Blueprint in `app/__init__.py`:

```python
from flask import Flask
from app.main.routes import main
from app.users.routes import users
from app.auth.routes import auth

def create_app():
    app = Flask(__name__)

    # Register Blueprints
    app.register_blueprint(main)
    app.register_blueprint(users)
    app.register_blueprint(auth)

    return app
```

4. Update the directory structure:

```
flask_api/
├── app/
│   ├── __init__.py
│   ├── main/
│   │   ├── __init__.py
│   │   └── routes.py
│   ├── users/
│   │   ├── __init__.py
│   │   └── routes.py
│   ├── auth/
│   │   ├── __init__.py
│   │   └── routes.py
│   └── config.py
├── run.py
```

5. Run the application:

```bash
python run.py
```

6. Test the login route with curl:

```bash
curl -X POST -H "Content-Type: application/json" -d '{"username": "admin", "password": "secret"}' http://127.0.0.1:5000/login
```

Using Blueprints in Flask provides a clean and modular way to structure your application, making it easier to manage and scale. This is particularly beneficial in mobile app development, where a well-organized API can significantly simplify both the development and maintenance process. By dividing your application into distinct components, you can keep your codebase clean, modular, and maintainable. This approach also makes it easier to collaborate with other developers, as each module can be developed and tested independently.

By following the structure and examples provided in this article, you can build a robust and scalable API for your mobile app using Flask and Blueprints.

Chapter 3

Working with Data in Flask: Requests, Responses, and JSON

Flask is a lightweight and flexible micro web framework for Python, commonly used for building web applications and APIs. When building APIs for mobile app development with Flask, it's essential to understand how to handle requests, generate responses, and work with JSON data. In this article, we'll explore these concepts with practical code examples.

Handling Requests

In Flask, incoming requests are represented by the `request` object, which provides access to various parts of the request, such as headers, data, and form parameters. Let's look at how to handle different types of requests:

GET Requests

GET requests are used to retrieve data from the server. In Flask, you can handle GET requests using the `@app.route` decorator:

```python
from flask import Flask, request, jsonify

app = Flask(__name__)

@app.route('/users', methods=['GET'])
def get_users():
    # Logic to retrieve user data
    users = [
        {'id': 1, 'name': 'Alice'},
        {'id': 2, 'name': 'Bob'},
        {'id': 3, 'name': 'Charlie'}
    ]
    return jsonify(users)

if __name__ == '__main__':
    app.run(debug=True)
```

In this example, we define a route `/users` that responds to GET requests by returning a JSON list of users.

POST Requests

POST requests are used to send data to the server, typically to create a new resource. You can handle POST requests in Flask like this:

```python
@app.route('/users', methods=['POST'])
def create_user():
    new_user = request.get_json()
    # Logic to create a new user
    return jsonify(new_user), 201
```

Here, we use `request.get_json()` to parse the JSON data sent in the request body. We then process the data to create a new user and return the created user with a 201 status code.

Other HTTP Methods

Similarly, you can handle other HTTP methods like PUT and DELETE by specifying them in the `methods` argument of the `@app.route` decorator.

Generating Responses

Flask provides several ways to generate responses, such as returning plain text, HTML, or JSON. Let's focus on JSON responses, which are commonly used in API development for mobile apps.

JSON Responses

You can return JSON responses using the `jsonify` function provided by Flask. It takes a Python dictionary or list and converts it into a JSON response:

```python
@app.route('/users', methods=['GET'])
def get_users():
    users = [
        {'id': 1, 'name': 'Alice'},
        {'id': 2, 'name': 'Bob'},
        {'id': 3, 'name': 'Charlie'}
    ]
    return jsonify(users)
```

In this example, the `users` list is converted into a JSON response and returned to the client.

Working with JSON Data

JSON (JavaScript Object Notation) is a lightweight data interchange format commonly used in web development, including API development. Flask makes it easy to work with JSON data both in request payloads and response bodies.

Parsing JSON Requests

To parse JSON data sent in a request body, you can use the `get_json()` method of the `request` object:

```python
@app.route('/users', methods=['POST'])
def create_user():
    new_user = request.get_json()
    # Process the JSON data to create a new user
    return jsonify(new_user), 201
```

Here, `request.get_json()` parses the JSON data sent in the request body and returns it as a Python dictionary.

Returning JSON Responses

To return JSON responses, you can use the `jsonify` function, as shown earlier. You can pass a Python dictionary or list to `jsonify`, and it will convert it into a JSON response:

```python
@app.route('/users', methods=['GET'])
def get_users():
```

```
    users = [
        {'id': 1, 'name': 'Alice'},
        {'id': 2, 'name': 'Bob'},
        {'id': 3, 'name': 'Charlie'}
    ]
    return jsonify(users)
```

This route returns a JSON response containing a list of user objects.

Error Handling

In API development, it's essential to handle errors gracefully and provide informative error messages to the client. Flask provides mechanisms for error handling, including returning appropriate HTTP status codes and error messages.

Returning Error Responses

You can return error responses with the appropriate HTTP status codes using `jsonify`. For example, to return a 404 Not Found error:

```python
@app.route('/users/<int:user_id>', methods=['GET'])
```

```
def get_user(user_id):
    user = find_user_by_id(user_id)
    if user is None:
        return jsonify({'error': 'User not found'}), 404
    return jsonify(user)
```

In this example, if the user with the specified ID is not found, we return a JSON response with an error message and a 404 status code.

Working with data in Flask APIs for mobile app development involves handling requests, generating responses, and working with JSON data. Flask provides convenient mechanisms for these tasks, including the `request` object for accessing request data, the `jsonify` function for generating JSON responses, and methods for parsing JSON data in requests. By understanding and leveraging these features, you can build robust and efficient APIs to support your mobile applications.

Integrating Databases with Flask (Popular Options and Connection)

Flask is a versatile web framework for Python that allows developers to build web applications and APIs quickly and efficiently. When developing APIs for mobile app development, integrating databases becomes essential for storing and managing data. In this article, we'll explore popular options for integrating databases with Flask and how to establish connections to these databases, along with code examples.

Popular Database Options

Flask supports a variety of database options, ranging from traditional relational databases to NoSQL databases. Some popular options include:

1. SQLite: A lightweight, serverless, and self-contained SQL database engine that's ideal for small to medium-sized applications.

2. MySQL: A popular open-source relational database management system (RDBMS) known for its speed, reliability, and scalability.

3. PostgreSQL: An advanced open-source object-relational database system known for its robust feature set, performance, and reliability.

4. MongoDB: A NoSQL document-oriented database that stores data in flexible, JSON-like documents, making it suitable for handling unstructured data.

Establishing Database Connections

Let's explore how to establish connections to SQLite, MySQL, and PostgreSQL databases in a Flask application.

SQLite

SQLite is the default database engine in Python, and it's straightforward to integrate with Flask. Here's how you can establish a connection to an SQLite database:

```python
import sqlite3
from flask import Flask

app = Flask(__name__)

@app.route('/')
def home():
    # Establish a connection to the SQLite database
    conn = sqlite3.connect('database.db')
    cursor = conn.cursor()

    # Execute SQL queries
    cursor.execute('SELECT * FROM users')
    users = cursor.fetchall()
```

```
    # Close the connection
    conn.close()

    return 'Number of users: ' + str(len(users))

if __name__ == '__main__':
    app.run(debug=True)
```

In this example, we import the `sqlite3` module, establish a connection to the SQLite database `database.db`, execute SQL queries using a cursor, fetch the results, and then close the connection.

MySQL

To connect Flask to a MySQL database, you'll need to install the `flask-mysql` package. Here's an example of how to establish a connection to a MySQL database:

```python
from flask import Flask
from flaskext.mysql import MySQL

app = Flask(__name__)
```

```python
# MySQL configurations
app.config['MYSQL_DATABASE_HOST'] = 'localhost'
app.config['MYSQL_DATABASE_USER'] = 'username'
app.config['MYSQL_DATABASE_PASSWORD'] = 'password'
app.config['MYSQL_DATABASE_DB'] = 'database'

mysql = MySQL()
mysql.init_app(app)

@app.route('/')
def home():
    # Establish a connection to the MySQL database
    conn = mysql.connect()
    cursor = conn.cursor()

    # Execute SQL queries
    cursor.execute('SELECT * FROM users')
    users = cursor.fetchall()

    # Close the connection
    conn.close()

    return 'Number of users: ' + str(len(users))

if __name__ == '__main__':
    app.run(debug=True)
```

```

In this example, we configure Flask to connect to a MySQL database, establish a connection using the `mysql.connect()` method, execute SQL queries using a cursor, fetch the results, and then close the connection.

**PostgreSQL**

To connect Flask to a PostgreSQL database, you'll need to install the `flask-sqlalchemy` package. Here's an example of how to establish a connection to a PostgreSQL database:

```python
from flask import Flask
from flask_sqlalchemy import SQLAlchemy

app = Flask(__name__)

# PostgreSQL configurations
app.config['SQLALCHEMY_DATABASE_URI'] = 'postgresql://username:password@localhost/database'

db = SQLAlchemy(app)

class User(db.Model):

```
    id = db.Column(db.Integer, primary_key=True)
    name = db.Column(db.String(50), nullable=False)

@app.route('/')
def home():
    # Execute SQL queries
    users = User.query.all()

    return 'Number of users: ' + str(len(users))

if __name__ == '__main__':
    app.run(debug=True)
```

In this example, we configure Flask to connect to a PostgreSQL database using SQLAlchemy, define a `User` model class representing a database table, execute SQL queries using SQLAlchemy's query interface, and fetch the results.

Integrating databases with Flask is essential for building robust APIs to support mobile app development. Flask supports a variety of database options, including SQLite, MySQL, and PostgreSQL, each with its strengths and use cases. By establishing connections to these databases and executing SQL queries or using ORM libraries like SQLAlchemy, you can store and manage data efficiently in your Flask applications. Choose the database option that best fits your application's requirements and start building powerful APIs for your mobile apps with Flask.

CRUD Operations (Create, Read, Update, Delete) with Flask and Databases

CRUD operations (Create, Read, Update, Delete) are fundamental to building APIs for mobile app development. In this article, we'll explore how to implement CRUD operations using Flask and databases, covering both SQL and NoSQL databases. We'll provide code examples for each operation, demonstrating how to interact with databases in a Flask application.

Setting Up Flask and Database

Before we dive into CRUD operations, let's set up a basic Flask application and choose a database. For demonstration purposes, we'll use SQLite for SQL-based operations and MongoDB for NoSQL-based operations.

SQLite Setup

First, install Flask and SQLite:

```bash
pip install Flask
```

```

## MongoDB Setup

For MongoDB, you'll need to install `pymongo`, the Python driver for MongoDB:

```bash
pip install pymongo
```

Creating a Flask Application

Let's create a basic Flask application with routes for CRUD operations.

```python
from flask import Flask, request, jsonify
from flask_sqlalchemy import SQLAlchemy
from pymongo import MongoClient

app = Flask(__name__)
app.config['SQLALCHEMY_DATABASE_URI'] = 'sqlite:///data.db'
db = SQLAlchemy(app)

# MongoDB connection

```
mongo_client = MongoClient('mongodb://localhost:27017')
mongo_db = mongo_client['flask_mongodb']
mongo_collection = mongo_db['items']

# SQLite Model
class Item(db.Model):
    id = db.Column(db.Integer, primary_key=True)
    name = db.Column(db.String(50), nullable=False)

# SQLite Table creation
db.create_all()

@app.route('/')
def home():
    return 'Welcome to Flask CRUD API'

if __name__ == '__main__':
    app.run(debug=True)
```
```

CRUD Operations

Now, let's implement CRUD operations for both SQLite and MongoDB databases.

Create Operation
```

```python
# SQLite Create Operation
@app.route('/sqlite/item', methods=['POST'])
def create_item_sqlite():
    data = request.json
    new_item = Item(name=data['name'])
    db.session.add(new_item)
    db.session.commit()
    return jsonify({'message': 'Item created successfully'}), 201

# MongoDB Create Operation
@app.route('/mongo/item', methods=['POST'])
def create_item_mongo():
    data = request.json
    mongo_collection.insert_one(data)
    return jsonify({'message': 'Item created successfully'}), 201
```

Read Operation

```python
# SQLite Read Operation
@app.route('/sqlite/items', methods=['GET'])
def get_items_sqlite():
```

```
    items = Item.query.all()
    return jsonify([{'id': item.id, 'name': item.name} for item in items])

# MongoDB Read Operation
@app.route('/mongo/items', methods=['GET'])
def get_items_mongo():
    items = list(mongo_collection.find({}, {'_id': False}))
    return jsonify(items)
```

Update Operation

```python
# SQLite Update Operation
@app.route('/sqlite/item/<int:item_id>', methods=['PUT'])
def update_item_sqlite(item_id):
    data = request.json
    item = Item.query.get_or_404(item_id)
    item.name = data['name']
    db.session.commit()
    return jsonify({'message': 'Item updated successfully'})

# MongoDB Update Operation
```

```python
@app.route('/mongo/item/<string:item_id>', methods=['PUT'])
def update_item_mongo(item_id):
    data = request.json
    mongo_collection.update_one({'_id': item_id}, {'$set': {'name': data['name']}})
    return jsonify({'message': 'Item updated successfully'})
```

Delete Operation

```python
# SQLite Delete Operation
@app.route('/sqlite/item/<int:item_id>', methods=['DELETE'])
def delete_item_sqlite(item_id):
    item = Item.query.get_or_404(item_id)
    db.session.delete(item)
    db.session.commit()
    return jsonify({'message': 'Item deleted successfully'})

# MongoDB Delete Operation
@app.route('/mongo/item/<string:item_id>', methods=['DELETE'])
def delete_item_mongo(item_id):
    mongo_collection.delete_one({'_id': item_id})
```

```
    return jsonify({'message': 'Item deleted successfully'})
```

In this article, we explored how to implement CRUD operations using Flask and databases, specifically SQLite and MongoDB. We covered how to set up a basic Flask application, define routes for CRUD operations, and interact with databases to perform Create, Read, Update, and Delete operations. By following these examples, you can build powerful APIs for mobile app development with Flask, allowing your applications to store, retrieve, update, and delete data efficiently.

User Authentication and Authorization for Secure Data Access in Flask API

User authentication and authorization are critical components of any web application, especially when developing APIs for mobile app development. In this article, we'll explore how to implement user authentication and authorization in a Flask API to ensure secure data access. We'll cover the concepts of authentication and authorization, provide code examples for implementing them in Flask, and discuss best practices for ensuring the security of your API.

Understanding Authentication and Authorization

Authentication is the process of verifying the identity of a user, typically by validating their credentials (e.g., username and password). Once a user is authenticated, they are issued a token or session that identifies them for subsequent requests.

Authorization, on the other hand, is the process of determining what actions a user is allowed to perform within the application or API. This involves checking the user's permissions or roles to ensure they have the necessary privileges to access certain resources or perform specific operations.

Implementing User Authentication with Flask

Flask provides various libraries and techniques for implementing user authentication. One common approach is to use JSON Web Tokens (JWT) for stateless authentication. Here's how you can implement user authentication using JWT in Flask:

```python
from flask import Flask, jsonify, request
import jwt
import datetime
```

```python
app = Flask(__name__)
app.config['SECRET_KEY'] = 'your_secret_key'

# User database (in memory for demonstration purposes)
users = {
    'admin': 'admin_password'
}

@app.route('/login', methods=['POST'])
def login():
    auth = request.authorization

    if not auth or not auth.username or not auth.password:
        return jsonify({'message': 'Authentication failed'}), 401

    if auth.username in users and users[auth.username] == auth.password:
        token = jwt.encode({'user': auth.username, 'exp': datetime.datetime.utcnow() + datetime.timedelta(minutes=30)}, app.config['SECRET_KEY'])
        return jsonify({'token': token.decode('UTF-8')})

    return jsonify({'message': 'Authentication failed'}), 401
```

```python
if __name__ == '__main__':
    app.run(debug=True)
```

In this example, we define a `/login` endpoint that accepts POST requests with username and password credentials. If the credentials are valid, a JWT token is generated and returned to the client.

Implementing User Authorization with Flask

Once a user is authenticated, you can implement authorization to restrict access to certain endpoints or resources based on the user's roles or permissions. Here's how you can implement authorization using Flask decorators:

```python
from functools import wraps
from flask import request, jsonify
import jwt

def token_required(f):
    @wraps(f)
    def decorated(*args, **kwargs):
        token = request.headers.get('Authorization')
```

```
    if not token:
        return jsonify({'message': 'Token is missing'}), 401

    try:
        data = jwt.decode(token, app.config['SECRET_KEY'])
        current_user = data['user']
    except:
        return jsonify({'message': 'Token is invalid'}), 401

    return f(current_user, *args, **kwargs)

  return decorated

@app.route('/protected')
@token_required
def protected(current_user):
    return jsonify({'message': 'Protected endpoint', 'current_user': current_user})
```

In this example, we define a `token_required` decorator that checks for the presence of a JWT token in the request headers. If a valid token is present, the decorator extracts the user information from the token and passes it to the decorated function. Otherwise, it returns a 401 Unauthorized error.

Best Practices for Secure User Authentication and Authorization

1. Use HTTPS: Always use HTTPS to encrypt communication between the client and server, preventing eavesdropping and man-in-the-middle attacks.

2. Store Passwords Securely: Hash passwords using strong cryptographic hashing algorithms (e.g., bcrypt) before storing them in the database.

3. Implement Token Expiration: Set expiration times for JWT tokens to limit their lifespan and reduce the risk of token misuse.

4. Use Refresh Tokens: Implement refresh tokens to allow users to obtain new access tokens without requiring them to re-enter their credentials.

5. Limit Access: Restrict access to sensitive endpoints or resources based on user roles or permissions to minimize the risk of unauthorized access.

6. Protect Against CSRF: Use anti-CSRF measures such as CSRF tokens to prevent cross-site request forgery attacks.

7. Implement Rate Limiting: Implement rate limiting to prevent brute-force attacks and limit the number of requests a user can make within a given time period.

8. Regularly Audit Access Logs: Monitor access logs regularly to detect and investigate any suspicious activity or unauthorized access attempts.

User authentication and authorization are essential components of building secure APIs for mobile app development. In this article, we explored how to implement user authentication and authorization in a Flask API using JSON Web Tokens (JWT) and decorators. By following best practices and implementing robust security measures, you can ensure that your API remains secure and protects sensitive user data from unauthorized access and misuse.

Chapter 4

Security Sentinel - Guarding Your Mobile App Fortress

User Authentication Best Practices (Sessions, Tokens) in Flask API

User authentication is a critical component in developing secure and reliable APIs for mobile applications. It ensures that only authorized users can access certain resources or perform specific actions. In Flask, user authentication can be implemented using sessions or tokens. Each method has its advantages and is suitable for different scenarios. This article will cover best practices for user authentication in Flask, focusing on sessions and tokens, and provide code examples to illustrate these concepts.

Sessions

Sessions are a server-side approach to maintaining user state. When a user logs in, the server generates a session ID, which is stored on the client-side (usually in a cookie). The server keeps a mapping of session IDs to user data. This method is simple and straightforward but requires the server to maintain state.

Implementing Sessions in Flask

Flask provides built-in support for sessions using cookies. Here's how you can implement user authentication using sessions:

1. Set Up Flask and Install Dependencies

```bash
pip install Flask Flask-Session Flask-SQLAlchemy
```

2. Create a Basic Flask App

```python
from flask import Flask, session, redirect, url_for, request, render_template, jsonify
from flask_sqlalchemy import SQLAlchemy
from flask_session import Session

app = Flask(__name__)
app.config['SECRET_KEY'] = 'supersecretkey'
app.config['SQLALCHEMY_DATABASE_URI'] = 'sqlite:///users.db'
app.config['SESSION_TYPE'] = 'filesystem'
db = SQLAlchemy(app)
```

```python
Session(app)

class User(db.Model):
    id = db.Column(db.Integer, primary_key=True)
    username = db.Column(db.String(50), unique=True, nullable=False)
    password = db.Column(db.String(50), nullable=False)

db.create_all()

@app.route('/register', methods=['POST'])
def register():
    data = request.json
    new_user = User(username=data['username'], password=data['password'])
    db.session.add(new_user)
    db.session.commit()
    return jsonify({'message': 'User registered successfully'})

@app.route('/login', methods=['POST'])
def login():
    data = request.json
    user = User.query.filter_by(username=data['username']).first()
    if user and user.password == data['password']:
        session['user_id'] = user.id
```

```
        return jsonify({'message': 'Login successful'})
    return jsonify({'message': 'Invalid credentials'}), 401

@app.route('/logout')
def logout():
    session.pop('user_id', None)
    return jsonify({'message': 'Logged out successfully'})

@app.route('/profile')
def profile():
    if 'user_id' in session:
        user = User.query.get(session['user_id'])
        return jsonify({'username': user.username})
    return jsonify({'message': 'Unauthorized'}), 401

if __name__ == '__main__':
    app.run(debug=True)
```
```

## Tokens

Tokens are a stateless approach to authentication, often used in modern web and mobile applications. JWT (JSON Web Tokens) is a popular method for token-based authentication. Tokens contain encoded information about the user and can be verified without maintaining server-side state.
```

Implementing Tokens in Flask

1. Set Up Flask and Install Dependencies

```bash
pip install Flask Flask-JWT-Extended Flask-SQLAlchemy
```

2. Create a Basic Flask App

```python
from flask import Flask, request, jsonify
from flask_sqlalchemy import SQLAlchemy
from flask_jwt_extended import JWTManager, create_access_token, jwt_required, get_jwt_identity

app = Flask(__name__)
app.config['SECRET_KEY'] = 'supersecretkey'
app.config['SQLALCHEMY_DATABASE_URI'] = 'sqlite:///users.db'
app.config['JWT_SECRET_KEY'] = 'anothersecretkey'
db = SQLAlchemy(app)
jwt = JWTManager(app)

class User(db.Model):
```

```python
    id = db.Column(db.Integer, primary_key=True)
    username = db.Column(db.String(50), unique=True, nullable=False)
    password = db.Column(db.String(50), nullable=False)

db.create_all()

@app.route('/register', methods=['POST'])
def register():
    data = request.json
    new_user = User(username=data['username'], password=data['password'])
    db.session.add(new_user)
    db.session.commit()
    return jsonify({'message': 'User registered successfully'})

@app.route('/login', methods=['POST'])
def login():
    data = request.json
    user = User.query.filter_by(username=data['username']).first()
    if user and user.password == data['password']:
        access_token = create_access_token(identity=user.username)
        return jsonify({'token': access_token})
    return jsonify({'message': 'Invalid credentials'}), 401
```

```python
@app.route('/profile')
@jwt_required()
def profile():
    current_user = get_jwt_identity()
    user = User.query.filter_by(username=current_user).first()
    return jsonify({'username': user.username})

if __name__ == '__main__':
    app.run(debug=True)
```

Best Practices for User Authentication

Sessions

1. Use Secure Cookies: Ensure cookies are secure and HTTP-only to prevent cross-site scripting (XSS) attacks.

```python
app.config['SESSION_COOKIE_SECURE'] = True
app.config['SESSION_COOKIE_HTTPONLY'] = True
```

2. Session Expiration: Implement session expiration to limit the time a session remains valid.

```python
from datetime import timedelta
app.config['PERMANENT_SESSION_LIFETIME'] = timedelta(minutes=30)
```

3. Store Minimal Information: Avoid storing sensitive information in the session. Use session IDs to reference user data stored securely on the server.

4. Regenerate Session IDs: Regenerate session IDs after login to prevent session fixation attacks.

```python
from flask import session
session.regenerate_id()
```

Tokens

1. Use Secure and Short-Lived Tokens: Keep tokens short-lived to reduce the risk of misuse.

```python
app.config['JWT_ACCESS_TOKEN_EXPIRES'] = timedelta(minutes=30)
```

```

**2. Use Refresh Tokens:** Implement refresh tokens to allow users to obtain new access tokens without re-authenticating.

```python
@app.route('/refresh', methods=['POST'])
@jwt_refresh_token_required
def refresh():
    current_user = get_jwt_identity()
    new_token = create_access_token(identity=current_user)
    return jsonify({'token': new_token})
```

3. Secure Token Storage: Ensure tokens are stored securely on the client side (e.g., in secure storage on mobile devices).

4. Token Revocation: Implement token revocation to invalidate tokens when necessary (e.g., on logout).

5. Use Strong Secret Keys: Use strong, random secret keys for signing tokens to prevent tampering.

```python

```
app.config['JWT_SECRET_KEY'] =
'anotherstrongsecretkey'
```
```

6. Validate Tokens on Every Request: Validate the token on every request to protected endpoints to ensure it is still valid and has not been tampered with.

User authentication is a fundamental aspect of securing your Flask API for mobile app development. Whether you choose sessions or tokens, it's crucial to follow best practices to ensure the security and reliability of your authentication system. Sessions are simple and suitable for smaller applications with server-side state management, while tokens (especially JWT) are ideal for stateless, scalable applications. By implementing secure authentication mechanisms and following best practices, you can protect your API and user data from unauthorized access and potential security threats.

Authorization Strategies: Role-Based Access Control (RBAC) in Flask API for Mobile App Development

In modern web and mobile applications, managing who can access specific resources and perform certain actions is critical for security and functionality. Role-Based
```

Access Control (RBAC) is a popular authorization strategy that simplifies permission management by assigning roles to users and associating permissions with those roles. This article will explore RBAC in the context of Flask API development for mobile apps, complete with code examples to demonstrate its implementation.

Understanding Role-Based Access Control (RBAC)

RBAC is an approach to restricting system access to authorized users based on their roles. Each role is assigned a set of permissions, and users are assigned roles based on their responsibilities and needs. The main benefits of RBAC include:

1. Simplicity: Managing permissions through roles is easier than assigning permissions to individual users.

2. Scalability: It scales well with large numbers of users and permissions.

3. Security: It helps ensure that users have the minimum necessary access rights.

Setting Up Flask for RBAC

To implement RBAC in a Flask API, we'll use `Flask-SQLAlchemy` for database interactions and `Flask-JWT-Extended` for authentication. Follow these steps:

1. Install Dependencies:

```bash
pip install Flask Flask-SQLAlchemy Flask-JWT-Extended
```

2. Set Up Flask App:

```python
from flask import Flask, request, jsonify
from flask_sqlalchemy import SQLAlchemy
from flask_jwt_extended import JWTManager, create_access_token, jwt_required, get_jwt_identity

app = Flask(__name__)
app.config['SECRET_KEY'] = 'supersecretkey'
app.config['SQLALCHEMY_DATABASE_URI'] = 'sqlite:///rbac.db'
app.config['JWT_SECRET_KEY'] = 'anothersecretkey'
db = SQLAlchemy(app)
jwt = JWTManager(app)
```

```
# Define User, Role, and Permission models
class User(db.Model):
    id = db.Column(db.Integer, primary_key=True)
    username = db.Column(db.String(50), unique=True, nullable=False)
    password = db.Column(db.String(50), nullable=False)
    role_id = db.Column(db.Integer, db.ForeignKey('role.id'), nullable=False)

class Role(db.Model):
    id = db.Column(db.Integer, primary_key=True)
    name = db.Column(db.String(50), unique=True, nullable=False)
    permissions = db.Column(db.String(200), nullable=False)  # Comma-separated permissions

# Initialize database
db.create_all()
```
```

## Implementing RBAC

### 1. Role and Permission Management

First, we define roles and associate them with permissions. For simplicity, permissions are stored as a comma-separated string in the `Role` model.
```

```python
# Sample roles and permissions
admin_role = Role(name='admin', permissions='create,read,update,delete')
user_role = Role(name='user', permissions='read')
db.session.add(admin_role)
db.session.add(user_role)
db.session.commit()
```

2. User Registration and Role Assignment

When registering users, we assign them roles.

```python
@app.route('/register', methods=['POST'])
def register():
    data = request.json
    role = Role.query.filter_by(name=data['role']).first()
    if not role:
        return jsonify({'message': 'Role not found'}), 400

    new_user = User(username=data['username'], password=data['password'], role_id=role.id)
    db.session.add(new_user)
    db.session.commit()
```

```
    return jsonify({'message': 'User registered successfully'}), 201
```

3. User Authentication

Upon successful login, a JWT token is generated for the user.

```python
@app.route('/login', methods=['POST'])
def login():
    data = request.json
    user = User.query.filter_by(username=data['username']).first()
    if user and user.password == data['password']:
        access_token = create_access_token(identity={'username': user.username, 'role': user.role.name})
        return jsonify({'token': access_token})
    return jsonify({'message': 'Invalid credentials'}), 401
```

4. Authorization Middleware

We create a decorator to check if the logged-in user has the required permissions to access a resource.

```python
from functools import wraps

def role_required(*required_permissions):
    def decorator(f):
        @wraps(f)
        def decorated_function(*args, **kwargs):
            current_user = get_jwt_identity()
            user = User.query.filter_by(username=current_user['username']).first()
            user_permissions = user.role.permissions.split(',')
            if any(permission in user_permissions for permission in required_permissions):
                return f(*args, **kwargs)
            return jsonify({'message': 'Access denied'}), 403
        return decorated_function
    return decorator
```

5. Protected Routes

Finally, we create routes that are protected by the `role_required` decorator.

```python
```

```python
@app.route('/create', methods=['POST'])
@jwt_required()
@role_required('create')
def create_item():
    data = request.json
    # Logic to create an item
    return jsonify({'message': 'Item created successfully'})

@app.route('/read', methods=['GET'])
@jwt_required()
@role_required('read')
def read_items():
    # Logic to read items
    return jsonify({'items': 'List of items'})

@app.route('/update', methods=['PUT'])
@jwt_required()
@role_required('update')
def update_item():
    data = request.json
    # Logic to update an item
    return jsonify({'message': 'Item updated successfully'})

@app.route('/delete', methods=['DELETE'])
@jwt_required()
@role_required('delete')
```

```
def delete_item():
    data = request.json
    # Logic to delete an item
    return jsonify({'message': 'Item deleted successfully'})
```
```

## Best Practices for RBAC in Flask

**1. Granular Permissions:** Define fine-grained permissions to control access to specific resources or actions. This makes it easier to grant and revoke access as needed.

**2. Least Privilege Principle:** Assign roles that provide the minimum necessary permissions for users to perform their tasks. This reduces the risk of unauthorized actions.

**3. Regular Role Audits:** Periodically review and update roles and permissions to ensure they align with current business requirements and security policies.

**4. Dynamic Role Management:** Implement functionality to add, modify, and delete roles and permissions dynamically without requiring code changes. This can be achieved through an admin interface.
```

5. Logging and Monitoring: Keep logs of all access attempts and actions performed by users. This helps in auditing and identifying potential security breaches.

6. Scalable Role Hierarchy: Design a role hierarchy that allows for scalability. For instance, having roles like `super_admin`, `admin`, and `user` where higher roles inherit permissions from lower roles.

7. Testing: Regularly test your RBAC implementation to ensure that unauthorized access is properly restricted and authorized access is correctly granted.

Implementing Role-Based Access Control (RBAC) in a Flask API for mobile app development enhances security by managing user permissions through roles. By assigning roles to users and associating permissions with those roles, you can simplify permission management and ensure that users have the appropriate access rights. This article provided a comprehensive guide to implementing RBAC in Flask, complete with code examples for setting up roles, managing user authentication, and protecting routes with authorization checks. By following best practices, you can create a secure and scalable authorization system for your Flask API.

Securing API Endpoints from Malicious Attacks in Flask for Mobile App Development

In the world of mobile app development, APIs are the backbone of data exchange between the client and server. However, exposing endpoints can make APIs vulnerable to various malicious attacks. Securing these endpoints is crucial to protect sensitive data and ensure the integrity and reliability of your application. This article explores various strategies for securing API endpoints in Flask, complete with code examples.

Understanding Common API Attacks

Before diving into the defenses, it's essential to understand common types of API attacks:

1. SQL Injection: Malicious SQL statements are inserted into an entry field for execution.

2. Cross-Site Scripting (XSS): Attackers inject malicious scripts into content that is then delivered to other users.

3. Cross-Site Request Forgery (CSRF): Attackers trick users into performing actions on a web application where they are authenticated.

4. Distributed Denial of Service (DDoS): Overwhelming the API with a flood of requests to exhaust resources.

5. Man-in-the-Middle (MitM) Attacks: Intercepting communications between the client and server to eavesdrop or alter data.

6. Unauthorized Access: Exploiting vulnerabilities to gain access to resources without proper authorization.

Best Practices for Securing API Endpoints

1. Use HTTPS

Ensure that all communication between the client and server is encrypted using HTTPS. This prevents eavesdropping and MitM attacks.

```python
from flask import Flask, request, jsonify
app = Flask(__name__)

@app.before_request
def before_request():
    if not request.is_secure:
```

```
    return jsonify({'message': 'Connection not secure'}),
403
```

```
@app.route('/secure-data', methods=['GET'])
def secure_data():
    return jsonify({'message': 'This is a secure endpoint'})
```

2. Authentication and Authorization

Implement robust authentication and authorization mechanisms. JWT (JSON Web Tokens) are commonly used for stateless authentication.

```python
from flask_jwt_extended import JWTManager, create_access_token, jwt_required, get_jwt_identity

app.config['JWT_SECRET_KEY'] = 'supersecretkey'
jwt = JWTManager(app)

@app.route('/login', methods=['POST'])
def login():
    data = request.json
    if data['username'] == 'admin' and data['password'] == 'password':
```

```
        token = create_access_token(identity={'username': 'admin'})
        return jsonify({'token': token})
    return jsonify({'message': 'Invalid credentials'}), 401

@app.route('/protected', methods=['GET'])
@jwt_required()
def protected():
    current_user = get_jwt_identity()
    return jsonify({'logged_in_as': current_user['username']})
```

3. Input Validation and Sanitization

Validate and sanitize all inputs to prevent SQL injection and XSS attacks. Use parameterized queries with SQLAlchemy to prevent SQL injection.

```python
from sqlalchemy.exc import IntegrityError

@app.route('/add-user', methods=['POST'])
def add_user():
    data = request.json
    username = data.get('username')
    password = data.get('password')
```

```python
    if not username or not password:
        return jsonify({'message': 'Username and password are required'}), 400

    try:
        new_user = User(username=username, password=password)
        db.session.add(new_user)
        db.session.commit()
    except IntegrityError:
        return jsonify({'message': 'User already exists'}), 409

    return jsonify({'message': 'User added successfully'}), 201
```

4. Rate Limiting

Implement rate limiting to protect against DDoS attacks and brute force attempts.

```python
from flask_limiter import Limiter
from flask_limiter.util import get_remote_address
```

```
limiter = Limiter(app, key_func=get_remote_address)

@app.route('/rate-limited', methods=['GET'])
@limiter.limit("5 per minute")
def rate_limited():
    return jsonify({'message': 'This endpoint is rate limited'})
```

5. CSRF Protection

Enable CSRF protection to prevent cross-site request forgery attacks.

```python
from flask_wtf.csrf import CSRFProtect

csrf = CSRFProtect(app)

@app.route('/form', methods=['POST'])
@csrf.exempt
def handle_form():
    data = request.form
    return jsonify({'message': 'Form data received'})
```

6. Logging and Monitoring

Set up logging and monitoring to detect suspicious activities and respond to potential threats.

```python
import logging

logging.basicConfig(level=logging.INFO)
logger = logging.getLogger(__name__)

@app.after_request
def log_request(response):
    logger.info(f"{request.remote_addr} {request.method} {request.path} {response.status_code}")
    return response
```

7. Content Security Policy (CSP)

Implement CSP headers to prevent XSS attacks.

```python
@app.after_request
def set_csp(response):
    response.headers['Content-Security-Policy'] = "default-src 'self'"
```

```
    return response
```

8. Use Secure Headers

Set various HTTP headers to enhance security.

```python
from flask_talisman import Talisman

Talisman(app, content_security_policy=None)

@app.route('/secure-headers', methods=['GET'])
def secure_headers():
    return jsonify({'message': 'Secure headers applied'})
```

Putting It All Together: A Secure Flask API

Here's a comprehensive example combining these best practices into a secure Flask API:

```python
from flask import Flask, request, jsonify
from flask_sqlalchemy import SQLAlchemy
from flask_jwt_extended import JWTManager, create_access_token, jwt_required, get_jwt_identity
```

```python
from flask_limiter import Limiter
from flask_limiter.util import get_remote_address
from flask_wtf.csrf import CSRFProtect
from flask_talisman import Talisman
import logging

app = Flask(__name__)
app.config['SECRET_KEY'] = 'supersecretkey'
app.config['SQLALCHEMY_DATABASE_URI'] = 'sqlite:///secure_app.db'
app.config['JWT_SECRET_KEY'] = 'anothersecretkey'
app.config['SESSION_COOKIE_SECURE'] = True
app.config['SESSION_COOKIE_HTTPONLY'] = True

db = SQLAlchemy(app)
jwt = JWTManager(app)
limiter = Limiter(app, key_func=get_remote_address)
csrf = CSRFProtect(app)
Talisman(app, content_security_policy=None)

logging.basicConfig(level=logging.INFO)
logger = logging.getLogger(__name__)

class User(db.Model):
    id = db.Column(db.Integer, primary_key=True)
    username = db.Column(db.String(50), unique=True, nullable=False)
```

```python
    password = db.Column(db.String(50), nullable=False)

db.create_all()

@app.before_request
def before_request():
    if not request.is_secure:
        return jsonify({'message': 'Connection not secure'}), 403

@app.route('/register', methods=['POST'])
def register():
    data = request.json
    username = data.get('username')
    password = data.get('password')

    if not username or not password:
        return jsonify({'message': 'Username and password are required'}), 400

    try:
        new_user = User(username=username, password=password)
        db.session.add(new_user)
        db.session.commit()
    except IntegrityError:
```

```
    return jsonify({'message': 'User already exists'}), 409

   return jsonify({'message': 'User registered successfully'}), 201

@app.route('/login', methods=['POST'])
def login():
   data = request.json
   user = User.query.filter_by(username=data['username']).first()
   if user and user.password == data['password']:
      token = create_access_token(identity={'username': user.username})
      return jsonify({'token': token})
   return jsonify({'message': 'Invalid credentials'}), 401

@app.route('/protected', methods=['GET'])
@jwt_required()
def protected():
   current_user = get_jwt_identity()
   return jsonify({'logged_in_as': current_user['username']})

@app.route('/rate-limited', methods=['GET'])
@limiter.limit("5 per minute")
def rate_limited():
```

```
    return jsonify({'message': 'This endpoint is rate limited'})

@app.after_request
def log_request(response):
    logger.info(f"{request.remote_addr} {request.method} {request.path} {response.status_code}")
    return response

@app.after_request
def set_csp(response):
    response.headers['Content-Security-Policy'] = "default-src 'self'"
    return response

if __name__ == '__main__':
    app.run(debug=True, ssl_context=('cert.pem', 'key.pem'))
```

Securing API endpoints is a multifaceted task that requires a combination of various strategies and best practices. By implementing HTTPS, robust authentication and authorization, input validation, rate limiting, CSRF protection, logging, and secure headers, you can significantly enhance the security of your Flask

API for mobile app development. Regularly review and update your security measures to stay ahead of potential threats and ensure the safety and reliability of your application.

Data Encryption and Security Considerations for Mobile Apps Using Flask API

In the realm of mobile app development, securing data is paramount to protect user information from unauthorized access and potential breaches. This article delves into the best practices for data encryption and security considerations when developing mobile apps with Flask APIs. We'll cover various encryption techniques, secure data storage methods, and code examples to illustrate these concepts.

Importance of Data Encryption

Data encryption converts data into a coded form that can only be accessed by authorized users with the decryption key. It ensures data confidentiality and integrity, both in transit and at rest. Encryption is crucial for:

1. Protecting Sensitive Information: User credentials, personal information, and payment details must be encrypted to prevent unauthorized access.

2. Compliance: Many regulations, such as GDPR and HIPAA, mandate encryption to protect user data.

3. Maintaining Trust: Securing data builds trust with users, which is essential for the success of any mobile app.

Types of Encryption

1. Symmetric Encryption: The same key is used for both encryption and decryption. It's fast and suitable for encrypting large amounts of data.

2. Asymmetric Encryption: Uses a pair of keys (public and private). The public key encrypts the data, and the private key decrypts it. It's more secure but slower than symmetric encryption.

3. Hashing: Converts data into a fixed-length hash value. It's a one-way process used for securely storing passwords.

Implementing Data Encryption in Flask

1. Setting Up Flask and Dependencies

First, install Flask and the necessary libraries for encryption.

```bash
pip install Flask cryptography
```

2. Symmetric Encryption

We'll use the `cryptography` library for symmetric encryption. Here's a basic example:

```python
from flask import Flask, request, jsonify
from cryptography.fernet import Fernet

app = Flask(__name__)

# Generate a key for symmetric encryption
key = Fernet.generate_key()
cipher_suite = Fernet(key)

@app.route('/encrypt', methods=['POST'])
def encrypt_data():
    data = request.json.get('data')
    if not data:
        return jsonify({'message': 'No data provided'}), 400
```

```
    encrypted_data = cipher_suite.encrypt(data.encode())
    return jsonify({'encrypted_data': encrypted_data.decode()})

@app.route('/decrypt', methods=['POST'])
def decrypt_data():
    encrypted_data = request.json.get('encrypted_data')
    if not encrypted_data:
        return jsonify({'message': 'No encrypted data provided'}), 400

    decrypted_data = cipher_suite.decrypt(encrypted_data.encode())
    return jsonify({'decrypted_data': decrypted_data.decode()})

if __name__ == '__main__':
    app.run(debug=True)
```

3. Asymmetric Encryption

Asymmetric encryption can be used for secure key exchange. Here's an example using RSA from the `cryptography` library:

```python
from cryptography.hazmat.primitives.asymmetric import rsa, padding
from cryptography.hazmat.primitives import serialization, hashes

# Generate RSA keys
private_key = rsa.generate_private_key(
    public_exponent=65537,
    key_size=2048
)
public_key = private_key.public_key()

# Serialize keys for storage or transmission
pem_private_key = private_key.private_bytes(
    encoding=serialization.Encoding.PEM,
    format=serialization.PrivateFormat.PKCS8,
    encryption_algorithm=serialization.NoEncryption()
)

pem_public_key = public_key.public_bytes(
    encoding=serialization.Encoding.PEM,
    format=serialization.PublicFormat.SubjectPublicKeyInfo
)

@app.route('/encrypt', methods=['POST'])
```

```python
def encrypt_data():
    data = request.json.get('data')
    if not data:
        return jsonify({'message': 'No data provided'}), 400

    encrypted_data = public_key.encrypt(
        data.encode(),
        padding.OAEP(
            mgf=padding.MGF1(algorithm=hashes.SHA256()),
            algorithm=hashes.SHA256(),
            label=None
        )
    )
    return jsonify({'encrypted_data': encrypted_data.hex()})

@app.route('/decrypt', methods=['POST'])
def decrypt_data():
    encrypted_data = bytes.fromhex(request.json.get('encrypted_data'))
    if not encrypted_data:
        return jsonify({'message': 'No encrypted data provided'}), 400

    decrypted_data = private_key.decrypt(
        encrypted_data,
        padding.OAEP(
```

```
    mgf=padding.MGF1(algorithm=hashes.SHA256()),
        algorithm=hashes.SHA256(),
        label=None
    )
    return jsonify({'decrypted_data':
decrypted_data.decode()})

if __name__ == '__main__':
    app.run(debug=True)
```

Secure Data Storage

When dealing with sensitive data, it's essential to secure data both in transit and at rest.

1. Secure Storage in Mobile Apps

- **iOS**: Use the Keychain Services API for secure storage of sensitive information such as user credentials and tokens.

- **Android**: Use the `SharedPreferences` with encrypted storage provided by the `Jetpack Security` library.

```java
// Example in Android using EncryptedSharedPreferences
EncryptedSharedPreferences sharedPreferences = EncryptedSharedPreferences.create(
    "secure_prefs",

MasterKeys.getOrCreate(MasterKeys.AES256_GCM_SPEC),
    context,

EncryptedSharedPreferences.PrefKeyEncryptionScheme.AES256_SIV,

EncryptedSharedPreferences.PrefValueEncryptionScheme.AES256_GCM
);
SharedPreferences.Editor editor = sharedPreferences.edit();
editor.putString("token", "your_token");
editor.apply();
```

2. Database Encryption

For sensitive data stored in the database, encryption should be implemented at the application level.

Using SQLAlchemy with Flask:

```python
from sqlalchemy import create_engine, Column, Integer, String
from sqlalchemy.ext.declarative import declarative_base
from sqlalchemy.orm import sessionmaker
from cryptography.fernet import Fernet

# Set up database
Base = declarative_base()
engine = create_engine('sqlite:///secure_app.db')
Session = sessionmaker(bind=engine)
session = Session()

# Encryption key
key = Fernet.generate_key()
cipher_suite = Fernet(key)

class User(Base):
    __tablename__ = 'users'
    id = Column(Integer, primary_key=True)
    username = Column(String, unique=True)
    password = Column(String)

    def set_password(self, password):
```

```
        self.password =
cipher_suite.encrypt(password.encode()).decode()

    def check_password(self, password):
        return
cipher_suite.decrypt(self.password.encode()).decode()
== password

Base.metadata.create_all(engine)

# Usage example
new_user = User(username='admin')
new_user.set_password('password123')
session.add(new_user)
session.commit()

stored_user =
session.query(User).filter_by(username='admin').first()
assert stored_user.check_password('password123')
```
```

## Security Considerations

### 1. HTTPS for Data Transmission

Always use HTTPS to encrypt data in transit. This prevents eavesdropping and tampering.
```

2. Token-Based Authentication

Use tokens, such as JWTs, for stateless authentication. Ensure tokens are securely stored on the client side.

```python
from flask_jwt_extended import JWTManager, create_access_token, jwt_required, get_jwt_identity

app.config['JWT_SECRET_KEY'] = 'supersecretkey'
jwt = JWTManager(app)

@app.route('/login', methods=['POST'])
def login():
    data = request.json
    user = session.query(User).filter_by(username=data['username']).first()
    if user and user.check_password(data['password']):
        token = create_access_token(identity={'username': user.username})
        return jsonify({'token': token})
    return jsonify({'message': 'Invalid credentials'}), 401
```

3. Rate Limiting

Implement rate limiting to protect against brute-force attacks.

```python
from flask_limiter import Limiter
from flask_limiter.util import get_remote_address

limiter = Limiter(app, key_func=get_remote_address)

@app.route('/login', methods=['POST'])
@limiter.limit("5 per minute")
def login():
    data = request.json
    user = session.query(User).filter_by(username=data['username']).first()
    if user and user.check_password(data['password']):
        token = create_access_token(identity={'username': user.username})
        return jsonify({'token': token})
    return jsonify({'message': 'Invalid credentials'}), 401
```

4. Input Validation and Sanitization

Always validate and sanitize user inputs to prevent SQL injection and other injection attacks.

```python
@app.route('/register', methods=['POST'])
def register():
    data = request.json
    username = data.get('username')
    password = data.get('password')

    if not username or not password:
        return jsonify({'message': 'Username and password are required'}), 400

    try:
        new_user = User(username=username, password=password)
        db.session.add(new_user)
        db.session.commit()
    except IntegrityError:
        return jsonify({'message': 'User already exists'}), 409

    return jsonify({'message': 'User registered successfully'}), 201
```

5. CSRF Protection

Enable CSRF protection for forms and critical endpoints to prevent unauthorized actions.

```python
from flask_wtf.csrf import CSRFProtect

csrf = CSRFProtect(app)

@app.route('/form', methods=['POST'])
@csrf.exempt
def handle_form():
    data = request.form
    return jsonify({'message': 'Form data received'})
```

Securing data in mobile app development using Flask APIs requires a comprehensive approach that includes encryption, secure data storage, and robust security practices. By implementing encryption for both data in transit and at rest, validating and sanitizing inputs, enforcing strong authentication and authorization mechanisms, and incorporating additional security measures like rate limiting and CSRF protection, you can significantly enhance the security of your mobile app.

Comprehensive Example of a Secure Flask API

Let's consolidate the discussed concepts into a comprehensive Flask API that demonstrates best practices for data encryption and security.

Setup

First, ensure you have all the required libraries installed:

```bash
pip install Flask SQLAlchemy cryptography flask_jwt_extended flask_limiter flask_wtf
```

Flask Application

Here's a full example of a secure Flask API with user registration, login, and protected routes:

```python
from flask import Flask, request, jsonify
from flask_sqlalchemy import SQLAlchemy
from flask_jwt_extended import JWTManager, create_access_token, jwt_required, get_jwt_identity
from flask_limiter import Limiter
```

```python
from flask_limiter.util import get_remote_address
from flask_wtf.csrf import CSRFProtect
from cryptography.fernet import Fernet
import logging

app = Flask(__name__)

# Configuration
app.config['SECRET_KEY'] = 'supersecretkey'
app.config['SQLALCHEMY_DATABASE_URI'] = 'sqlite:///secure_app.db'
app.config['JWT_SECRET_KEY'] = 'anothersecretkey'
app.config['SESSION_COOKIE_SECURE'] = True
app.config['SESSION_COOKIE_HTTPONLY'] = True

# Initialize extensions
db = SQLAlchemy(app)
jwt = JWTManager(app)
limiter = Limiter(app, key_func=get_remote_address)
csrf = CSRFProtect(app)

# Logging
logging.basicConfig(level=logging.INFO)
logger = logging.getLogger(__name__)

# Encryption key for symmetric encryption
encryption_key = Fernet.generate_key()
```

```python
cipher_suite = Fernet(encryption_key)

# Database model
class User(db.Model):
    id = db.Column(db.Integer, primary_key=True)
    username = db.Column(db.String(50), unique=True, nullable=False)
    password = db.Column(db.String(200), nullable=False)

    def set_password(self, password):
        self.password = cipher_suite.encrypt(password.encode()).decode()

    def check_password(self, password):
        return cipher_suite.decrypt(self.password.encode()).decode() == password

# Create database tables
db.create_all()

# HTTPS Enforcement
@app.before_request
def before_request():
    if not request.is_secure:
```

```python
    return jsonify({'message': 'Connection not secure'}), 403

# User registration endpoint
@app.route('/register', methods=['POST'])
def register():
    data = request.json
    username = data.get('username')
    password = data.get('password')

    if not username or not password:
        return jsonify({'message': 'Username and password are required'}), 400

    try:
        new_user = User(username=username)
        new_user.set_password(password)
        db.session.add(new_user)
        db.session.commit()
    except IntegrityError:
        return jsonify({'message': 'User already exists'}), 409

    return jsonify({'message': 'User registered successfully'}), 201

# User login endpoint
```

```python
@app.route('/login', methods=['POST'])
@limiter.limit("5 per minute")
def login():
    data = request.json
    user = User.query.filter_by(username=data['username']).first()
    if user and user.check_password(data['password']):
        token = create_access_token(identity={'username': user.username})
        return jsonify({'token': token})
    return jsonify({'message': 'Invalid credentials'}), 401


# Protected endpoint
@app.route('/protected', methods=['GET'])
@jwt_required()
def protected():
    current_user = get_jwt_identity()
    return jsonify({'logged_in_as': current_user['username']})


# Data encryption endpoint
@app.route('/encrypt', methods=['POST'])
def encrypt_data():
    data = request.json.get('data')
    if not data:
        return jsonify({'message': 'No data provided'}), 400
```

```
    encrypted_data = cipher_suite.encrypt(data.encode())
    return jsonify({'encrypted_data': encrypted_data.decode()})

# Data decryption endpoint
@app.route('/decrypt', methods=['POST'])
def decrypt_data():
    encrypted_data = request.json.get('encrypted_data')
    if not encrypted_data:
        return jsonify({'message': 'No encrypted data provided'}), 400

    decrypted_data = cipher_suite.decrypt(encrypted_data.encode())
    return jsonify({'decrypted_data': decrypted_data.decode()})

# Logging requests
@app.after_request
def log_request(response):
    logger.info(f"{request.remote_addr} {request.method} {request.path} {response.status_code}")
    return response

# Content Security Policy
@app.after_request
```

```
def set_csp(response):
    response.headers['Content-Security-Policy'] = "default-src 'self'"
    return response

if __name__ == '__main__':
    app.run(debug=True, ssl_context=('cert.pem', 'key.pem'))
```
```

## Explanation

**1. Configuration and Initialization:**

- The Flask app is configured with essential settings, including secret keys for sessions and JWT.

- Extensions for SQLAlchemy, JWT, rate limiting, and CSRF protection are initialized.

- Logging is configured to monitor requests and responses.

**2. Encryption Key:**
```

- A symmetric encryption key is generated using the `cryptography` library.

3. Database Model:

- A `User` model is defined with methods to set and check passwords using symmetric encryption.

4. HTTPS Enforcement:

- A `before_request` handler ensures that all requests are made over HTTPS.

5. User Registration and Login:

- Endpoints for user registration and login are provided, including rate limiting on the login endpoint to mitigate brute-force attacks.

- Passwords are encrypted before storage in the database.

6. Protected Endpoint:

- A protected route requires a valid JWT token to access, ensuring that only authenticated users can reach it.

7. Data Encryption and Decryption Endpoints:

- Endpoints for encrypting and decrypting data demonstrate the use of symmetric encryption.

8. Logging and Content Security Policy:

- Requests and responses are logged for monitoring and auditing purposes.

- A content security policy header is set to mitigate XSS attacks.

Securing data in mobile app development with Flask APIs involves implementing multiple layers of security measures. Encryption, both symmetric and asymmetric, protects data at rest and in transit. Secure storage practices, robust authentication mechanisms, input validation, rate limiting, and other security headers collectively safeguard against a range of potential threats. By following these best practices and continually updating your security strategies, you can create a secure environment for your mobile app and its users.

Chapter 5

Why Testing Matters: Unit Testing and Integration Testing for Flask API in Mobile App Development

Testing is a critical component of software development, ensuring that code is reliable, secure, and performs as expected. In mobile app development, where APIs are integral to functionality, thorough testing can prevent costly errors, enhance user experience, and ensure the robustness of the application. This article delves into the importance of testing, focusing on unit testing and integration testing, and provides practical examples using Flask API.

Importance of Testing

1. Error Detection and Prevention

Testing helps identify bugs and issues early in the development cycle, making it easier and cheaper to fix them. Detecting errors before deployment reduces the risk of crashes and malfunctions in the production environment.

2. Code Quality and Maintainability

Well-tested code is often of higher quality. Unit tests ensure that individual components function correctly, while integration tests confirm that different parts of the system work together seamlessly. This results in more maintainable code, making it easier to implement new features and refactor existing code.

3. Documentation

Tests serve as a form of documentation. They provide examples of how different parts of the code are supposed to function, which can be invaluable for new developers joining the project.

4. Confidence in Changes

Having a robust suite of tests gives developers confidence when making changes to the codebase. They can refactor or add new features knowing that the existing functionality will not break if the tests pass.

Unit Testing

Unit testing involves testing individual components or units of code in isolation. In the context of a Flask API, this often means testing individual routes and functions to ensure they behave as expected.

Setting Up Unit Tests

1. Installing Required Libraries

First, install Flask and the testing libraries:

```bash
pip install Flask pytest pytest-flask
```

2. Creating a Simple Flask API

Here's a basic Flask API to demonstrate unit testing:

```python
from flask import Flask, jsonify, request

app = Flask(__name__)

@app.route('/add', methods=['GET'])
def add():
    a = request.args.get('a', type=int)
    b = request.args.get('b', type=int)
    result = a + b
```

```
    return jsonify({'result': result})

@app.route('/subtract', methods=['GET'])
def subtract():
    a = request.args.get('a', type=int)
    b = request.args.get('b', type=int)
    result = a - b
    return jsonify({'result': result})

if __name__ == '__main__':
    app.run(debug=True)
```

3. Writing Unit Tests

Create a `test_app.py` file for writing tests:

```python
import pytest
from app import app

@pytest.fixture
def client():
    with app.test_client() as client:
        yield client

def test_add(client):
```

```
    response = client.get('/add?a=2&b=3')
    json_data = response.get_json()
    assert response.status_code == 200
    assert json_data['result'] == 5

def test_subtract(client):
    response = client.get('/subtract?a=5&b=3')
    json_data = response.get_json()
    assert response.status_code == 200
    assert json_data['result'] == 2
```

4. Running Unit Tests

Run the tests using `pytest`:

```bash
pytest
```

Integration Testing

Integration testing involves testing how different components of the application work together. In the context of a Flask API, this means testing the interaction between routes, databases, and other external services.

Setting Up Integration Tests

1. Database Integration

Let's enhance our API to include a simple database operation using SQLAlchemy:

```bash
pip install flask_sqlalchemy
```

2. Updating the Flask API

Update the `app.py` to include a database:

```python
from flask import Flask, jsonify, request
from flask_sqlalchemy import SQLAlchemy

app = Flask(__name__)
app.config['SQLALCHEMY_DATABASE_URI'] = 'sqlite:///test.db'
db = SQLAlchemy(app)

class Item(db.Model):
    id = db.Column(db.Integer, primary_key=True)
```

```python
    name = db.Column(db.String(80), unique=True, nullable=False)
    price = db.Column(db.Float, nullable=False)

@app.route('/item', methods=['POST'])
def add_item():
    data = request.get_json()
    item = Item(name=data['name'], price=data['price'])
    db.session.add(item)
    db.session.commit()
    return jsonify({'message': 'Item added'}), 201

@app.route('/items', methods=['GET'])
def get_items():
    items = Item.query.all()
    return jsonify([{'name': item.name, 'price': item.price} for item in items])

if __name__ == '__main__':
    db.create_all()
    app.run(debug=True)
```

3. Writing Integration Tests

Create a new `test_integration.py` file:

```python
import pytest
from app import app, db, Item

@pytest.fixture
def client():
    app.config['TESTING'] = True
    app.config['SQLALCHEMY_DATABASE_URI'] = 'sqlite:///:memory:'
    with app.test_client() as client:
        with app.app_context():
            db.create_all()
        yield client

def test_add_item(client):
    response = client.post('/item', json={'name': 'Apple', 'price': 1.0})
    assert response.status_code == 201
    assert response.get_json() == {'message': 'Item added'}
    items = Item.query.all()
    assert len(items) == 1
    assert items[0].name == 'Apple'
    assert items[0].price == 1.0

def test_get_items(client):
    client.post('/item', json={'name': 'Apple', 'price': 1.0})
```

```
client.post('/item', json={'name': 'Banana', 'price': 0.5})
response = client.get('/items')
json_data = response.get_json()
assert response.status_code == 200
assert len(json_data) == 2
assert {'name': 'Apple', 'price': 1.0} in json_data
assert {'name': 'Banana', 'price': 0.5} in json_data
```

4. Running Integration Tests

Run the tests using `pytest`:

```bash
pytest
```

Best Practices for Testing

1. Isolation: Ensure unit tests are isolated. They should not depend on the state of the system or other tests. Use fixtures to set up and tear down the test environment.

2. Coverage: Aim for high test coverage but focus on critical and high-risk areas. Use tools like `pytest-cov` to measure coverage.

3. Consistent Environment: Run tests in a consistent environment. Use continuous integration (CI) services like GitHub Actions, Travis CI, or Jenkins to automate testing.

4. Performance: Ensure tests run quickly to keep the feedback loop short. Optimize test performance by mocking external services and databases when appropriate.

5. Meaningful Assertions: Write meaningful assertions that check not only the expected results but also edge cases and potential error conditions.

6. Maintainability: Keep tests clean and maintainable. Refactor test code as needed and avoid duplication.

Testing is an essential part of developing a reliable and maintainable Flask API for mobile applications. Unit testing ensures that individual components work correctly, while integration testing verifies that different parts of the system function together seamlessly. By following best practices and leveraging tools like `pytest`, you can build a robust testing suite that enhances code quality, prevents bugs, and facilitates confident changes to the codebase. Implementing thorough testing practices ultimately leads to a more secure, performant, and user-friendly application.

Setting Up a Testing Environment for Flask Applications

Setting up a robust testing environment for Flask applications is critical for ensuring the reliability, security, and performance of your application, particularly in the context of mobile app development where APIs play a crucial role. This guide will walk you through the process of setting up a comprehensive testing environment for Flask applications, covering the necessary tools and best practices.

Why a Testing Environment Matters

A proper testing environment allows you to:

1. Identify and fix bugs early in the development cycle.

2. Ensure that individual components (units) of your application function correctly.

3. Verify that integrated components work together as expected.

4. Maintain high code quality and improve maintainability.

5. Provide a safety net for refactoring and adding new features.

Setting Up Your Testing Environment

Prerequisites

Ensure you have Python and Flask installed. If not, install them using the following commands:

```bash
pip install Flask
```

Installing Testing Libraries

We'll use `pytest`, `pytest-flask`, and `pytest-cov` for our testing framework and coverage reporting:

```bash
pip install pytest pytest-flask pytest-cov
```

Creating a Simple Flask Application

Let's start with a simple Flask application to test. Create a file named `app.py`:

```python
from flask import Flask, jsonify, request

app = Flask(__name__)

@app.route('/add', methods=['GET'])
def add():
    a = request.args.get('a', type=int)
    b = request.args.get('b', type=int)
    result = a + b
    return jsonify({'result': result})

@app.route('/subtract', methods=['GET'])
def subtract():
    a = request.args.get('a', type=int)
    b = request.args.get('b', type=int)
    result = a - b
    return jsonify({'result': result})

if __name__ == '__main__':
    app.run(debug=True)
```

Writing Unit Tests

Unit tests focus on individual units of code, such as functions or methods, to ensure they work as expected.

Creating Test Directory and File

Create a `tests` directory and a `test_app.py` file:

```bash
mkdir tests
touch tests/test_app.py
```

Writing Unit Tests

In `tests/test_app.py`, write unit tests for the `add` and `subtract` endpoints:

```python
import pytest
from app import app

@pytest.fixture
def client():
    with app.test_client() as client:
        yield client
```

```
def test_add(client):
    response = client.get('/add?a=2&b=3')
    json_data = response.get_json()
    assert response.status_code == 200
    assert json_data['result'] == 5

def test_subtract(client):
    response = client.get('/subtract?a=5&b=3')
    json_data = response.get_json()
    assert response.status_code == 200
    assert json_data['result'] == 2
```

Running Unit Tests

Run the tests using `pytest`:

```bash
pytest
```

Setting Up Database for Integration Tests

Integration tests focus on the interactions between different parts of the application, such as database operations.

Installing SQLAlchemy

Install SQLAlchemy for database operations:

```bash
pip install flask_sqlalchemy
```

Updating Flask Application with Database

Update `app.py` to include a simple database model and endpoints:

```python
from flask import Flask, jsonify, request
from flask_sqlalchemy import SQLAlchemy

app = Flask(__name__)
app.config['SQLALCHEMY_DATABASE_URI'] = 'sqlite:///test.db'
db = SQLAlchemy(app)

class Item(db.Model):
    id = db.Column(db.Integer, primary_key=True)
    name = db.Column(db.String(80), unique=True, nullable=False)
```

```python
    price = db.Column(db.Float, nullable=False)

@app.route('/item', methods=['POST'])
def add_item():
    data = request.get_json()
    item = Item(name=data['name'], price=data['price'])
    db.session.add(item)
    db.session.commit()
    return jsonify({'message': 'Item added'}), 201

@app.route('/items', methods=['GET'])
def get_items():
    items = Item.query.all()
    return jsonify([{'name': item.name, 'price': item.price} for item in items])

if __name__ == '__main__':
    db.create_all()
    app.run(debug=True)
```

Writing Integration Tests

Create a new `test_integration.py` file in the `tests` directory:

```bash
```

```
touch tests/test_integration.py
```

Writing Integration Tests

In `tests/test_integration.py`, write integration tests for the `add_item` and `get_items` endpoints:

```python
import pytest
from app import app, db, Item

@pytest.fixture
def client():
    app.config['TESTING'] = True
    app.config['SQLALCHEMY_DATABASE_URI'] = 'sqlite:///:memory:'
    with app.test_client() as client:
        with app.app_context():
            db.create_all()
        yield client

def test_add_item(client):
    response = client.post('/item', json={'name': 'Apple', 'price': 1.0})
    assert response.status_code == 201
```

```
    assert response.get_json() == {'message': 'Item added'}
    items = Item.query.all()
    assert len(items) == 1
    assert items[0].name == 'Apple'
    assert items[0].price == 1.0

def test_get_items(client):
    client.post('/item', json={'name': 'Apple', 'price': 1.0})
    client.post('/item', json={'name': 'Banana', 'price': 0.5})
    response = client.get('/items')
    json_data = response.get_json()
    assert response.status_code == 200
    assert len(json_data) == 2
    assert {'name': 'Apple', 'price': 1.0} in json_data
    assert {'name': 'Banana', 'price': 0.5} in json_data
```

Running Integration Tests

Run the tests using `pytest`:

```bash
pytest
```

Code Coverage

To measure code coverage, use `pytest-cov`. Add the following to your `pytest` command:

```bash
pytest --cov=app tests/
```

This command generates a coverage report, showing which parts of your code are covered by tests.

Continuous Integration (CI)

Integrate testing into your CI pipeline to automatically run tests on code commits. Here's an example using GitHub Actions.

Setting Up GitHub Actions

Create a `.github/workflows/test.yml` file:

```yaml
name: Flask API Tests

on: [push, pull_request]

jobs:
```

```yaml
test:
  runs-on: ubuntu-latest

  steps:
  - uses: actions/checkout@v2

  - name: Set up Python
    uses: actions/setup-python@v2
    with:
      python-version: '3.8'

  - name: Install dependencies
    run: |
      python -m pip install --upgrade pip
      pip install Flask pytest pytest-flask pytest-cov flask_sqlalchemy

  - name: Run tests
    run: |
      pytest --cov=app tests/
```

Best Practices for Testing

1. Isolation: Ensure tests do not depend on the state of other tests. Use fixtures to set up and tear down the test environment.

2. Mocking External Services: Use mocking to simulate external services and dependencies, ensuring tests are fast and reliable.

3. Consistent Environment: Ensure tests run in a consistent environment. Use CI tools to automate testing and catch issues early.

4. Meaningful Assertions: Write meaningful assertions to verify both expected outcomes and edge cases.

5. Comprehensive Coverage: Aim for high test coverage, but focus on critical and high-risk areas of the codebase.

6. Performance: Ensure tests run quickly to maintain a fast feedback loop. Optimize test performance where possible.

Setting up a comprehensive testing environment for Flask applications is essential for ensuring the reliability, security, and performance of your application, particularly in mobile app development where APIs are crucial. By following best practices and using tools like `pytest`, `pytest-flask`, and `pytest-cov`, you can build a robust testing suite that enhances code quality and maintainability. Integrating testing into your CI pipeline further ensures that your application remains stable and reliable as it evolves.

Testing Flask Routes, Views, and Database Interactions

Testing Flask routes, views, and database interactions is crucial for ensuring the reliability and correctness of a Flask API, especially in mobile app development where APIs serve as the backbone for data exchange and functionality. This comprehensive guide will delve into the details of testing Flask routes, views, and database interactions with practical examples.

Importance of Testing

Testing ensures that:

1. Routes and Views Function Correctly: Each endpoint works as expected, returning the correct status codes and data.

2. Database Interactions Are Reliable: Database operations like creating, reading, updating, and deleting (CRUD) are correctly implemented.

3. Application Stability: The application can handle various edge cases and errors gracefully.

4. Code Quality: High-quality, maintainable code that can be confidently refactored and extended.

Setting Up Your Testing Environment

Before diving into the tests, ensure you have the necessary libraries installed:

```bash
pip install Flask pytest pytest-flask SQLAlchemy
```

Creating a Simple Flask Application

Let's start with a basic Flask application with routes and database interactions:

```python
# app.py
from flask import Flask, jsonify, request
from flask_sqlalchemy import SQLAlchemy

app = Flask(__name__)
```

```python
app.config['SQLALCHEMY_DATABASE_URI'] = 'sqlite:///test.db'
app.config['SQLALCHEMY_TRACK_MODIFICATIONS'] = False
db = SQLAlchemy(app)

class Item(db.Model):
    id = db.Column(db.Integer, primary_key=True)
    name = db.Column(db.String(80), unique=True, nullable=False)
    price = db.Column(db.Float, nullable=False)

@app.route('/item', methods=['POST'])
def add_item():
    data = request.get_json()
    if not data or not 'name' in data or not 'price' in data:
        return jsonify({'error': 'Bad Request'}), 400
    item = Item(name=data['name'], price=data['price'])
    db.session.add(item)
    db.session.commit()
    return jsonify({'message': 'Item added', 'item': {'name': item.name, 'price': item.price}}), 201

@app.route('/items', methods=['GET'])
def get_items():
    items = Item.query.all()
```

```python
    return jsonify([{'name': item.name, 'price': item.price}
for item in items])

@app.route('/item/<int:item_id>', methods=['GET'])
def get_item(item_id):
    item = Item.query.get_or_404(item_id)
    return jsonify({'name': item.name, 'price': item.price})

@app.route('/item/<int:item_id>', methods=['PUT'])
def update_item(item_id):
    data = request.get_json()
    item = Item.query.get_or_404(item_id)
    if 'name' in data:
        item.name = data['name']
    if 'price' in data:
        item.price = data['price']
    db.session.commit()
    return jsonify({'message': 'Item updated', 'item':
{'name': item.name, 'price': item.price}})

@app.route('/item/<int:item_id>', methods=['DELETE'])
def delete_item(item_id):
    item = Item.query.get_or_404(item_id)
    db.session.delete(item)
    db.session.commit()
    return jsonify({'message': 'Item deleted'})
```

```
if __name__ == '__main__':
    db.create_all()
    app.run(debug=True)
```

Writing Tests for Flask Routes, Views, and Database Interactions

Setting Up Test Directory and Files

Create a `tests` directory and a `test_app.py` file:

```bash
mkdir tests
touch tests/test_app.py
```

Writing Tests

In `tests/test_app.py`, we'll write tests for each route and database interaction.

```python
import pytest
from app import app, db, Item

@pytest.fixture
```

```python
def client():
    app.config['TESTING'] = True
    app.config['SQLALCHEMY_DATABASE_URI'] = 'sqlite:///:memory:'
    with app.test_client() as client:
        with app.app_context():
            db.create_all()
        yield client
        with app.app_context():
            db.drop_all()

def test_add_item(client):
    response = client.post('/item', json={'name': 'Apple', 'price': 1.0})
    json_data = response.get_json()
    assert response.status_code == 201
    assert json_data['message'] == 'Item added'
    assert json_data['item']['name'] == 'Apple'
    assert json_data['item']['price'] == 1.0

def test_get_items(client):
    client.post('/item', json={'name': 'Apple', 'price': 1.0})
    client.post('/item', json={'name': 'Banana', 'price': 0.5})
    response = client.get('/items')
    json_data = response.get_json()
    assert response.status_code == 200
    assert len(json_data) == 2
```

```python
    assert {'name': 'Apple', 'price': 1.0} in json_data
    assert {'name': 'Banana', 'price': 0.5} in json_data

def test_get_item(client):
    response = client.post('/item', json={'name': 'Apple', 'price': 1.0})
    item_id = response.get_json()['item']['id']
    response = client.get(f'/item/{item_id}')
    json_data = response.get_json()
    assert response.status_code == 200
    assert json_data['name'] == 'Apple'
    assert json_data['price'] == 1.0

def test_update_item(client):
    response = client.post('/item', json={'name': 'Apple', 'price': 1.0})
    item_id = response.get_json()['item']['id']
    response = client.put(f'/item/{item_id}', json={'name': 'Apple', 'price': 1.5})
    json_data = response.get_json()
    assert response.status_code == 200
    assert json_data['message'] == 'Item updated'
    assert json_data['item']['name'] == 'Apple'
    assert json_data['item']['price'] == 1.5

def test_delete_item(client):
```

```
    response = client.post('/item', json={'name': 'Apple', 'price': 1.0})
    item_id = response.get_json()['item']['id']
    response = client.delete(f'/item/{item_id}')
    json_data = response.get_json()
    assert response.status_code == 200
    assert json_data['message'] == 'Item deleted'
    response = client.get(f'/item/{item_id}')
    assert response.status_code == 404
```

Running Tests

Run the tests using `pytest`:

```bash
pytest
```

Detailed Explanation

Setting Up Test Client and Fixtures

The `client` fixture sets up the test client and configures the application for testing, using an in-memory SQLite database to ensure tests do not affect the production database.

```python
@pytest.fixture
def client():
    app.config['TESTING'] = True
    app.config['SQLALCHEMY_DATABASE_URI'] = 'sqlite:///:memory:'
    with app.test_client() as client:
        with app.app_context():
            db.create_all()
        yield client
        with app.app_context():
            db.drop_all()
```

This fixture:

1. Configures the app for testing by setting `TESTING` to `True`.

2. Uses an in-memory SQLite database for testing.

3. Creates the database schema before running tests and drops the schema after tests.

Testing Each Route

1. Add Item:

```python
def test_add_item(client):
    response = client.post('/item', json={'name': 'Apple', 'price': 1.0})
    json_data = response.get_json()
    assert response.status_code == 201
    assert json_data['message'] == 'Item added'
    assert json_data['item']['name'] == 'Apple'
    assert json_data['item']['price'] == 1.0
```

This test:

- Send a POST request to add a new item.

- Assert the response status code is 201.

- Checks that the response JSON contains the correct item details.

2. Get Items:

```python
def test_get_items(client):
    client.post('/item', json={'name': 'Apple', 'price': 1.0})
```

```
    client.post('/item', json={'name': 'Banana', 'price': 0.5})
    response = client.get('/items')
    json_data = response.get_json()
    assert response.status_code == 200
    assert len(json_data) == 2
    assert {'name': 'Apple', 'price': 1.0} in json_data
    assert {'name': 'Banana', 'price': 0.5} in json_data
```

This test:

- Adds two items.

- Sends a GET request to retrieve all items.

- Assert the response status code is 200.

- Checks that the response JSON contains both items.

3. Get Single Item:

```python
def test_get_item(client):
    response = client.post('/item', json={'name': 'Apple', 'price': 1.0})
    item_id = response.get_json()['item']['id']
```

```python
    response = client.get(f'/item/{item_id}')
    json_data = response.get_json()
    assert response.status_code == 200
    assert json_data['name'] == 'Apple'
    assert json_data['price'] == 1.0
```

This test:

- Adds an item and retrieves its ID.

- Sends a GET request to retrieve the item by ID.

- Assert the response status code is 200.

- Checks that the response JSON contains the correct details of the item.

4. Update Item:

```python
def test_update_item(client):
    response = client.post('/item', json={'name': 'Apple', 'price': 1.0})
    item_id = response.get_json()['item']['id']
    response = client.put(f'/item/{item_id}', json={'name': 'Apple', 'price': 1.5})
```

```
    json_data = response.get_json()
    assert response.status_code == 200
    assert json_data['message'] == 'Item updated'
    assert json_data['item']['name'] == 'Apple'
    assert json_data['item']['price'] == 1.5
```

This test:

- Adds an item and retrieves its ID.

- Sends a PUT request to update the item's details.

- Assert the response status code is 200.

- Checks that the response JSON confirms the update and contains the correct updated details.

5. Delete Item:

```python
def test_delete_item(client):
    response = client.post('/item', json={'name': 'Apple', 'price': 1.0})
    item_id = response.get_json()['item']['id']
    response = client.delete(f'/item/{item_id}')
    json_data = response.get_json()
```

```
    assert response.status_code == 200
    assert json_data['message'] == 'Item deleted'
    response = client.get(f'/item/{item_id}')
    assert response.status_code == 404
```

This test:

- Adds an item and retrieves its ID.

- Sends a DELETE request to remove the item.

- Assert the response status code is 200.

- Checks that the response JSON confirms the deletion.

- Verifies that a subsequent GET request for the deleted item returns a 404 status.

Running the Tests

Run all the tests using `pytest`:

```bash
pytest
```

Enhancing Tests with Additional Assertions and Edge Cases

To ensure comprehensive testing, consider adding more assertions and tests for edge cases:

1. Test Adding Item with Missing Data:

```python
def test_add_item_missing_data(client):
    response = client.post('/item', json={'name': 'Apple'})
    json_data = response.get_json()
    assert response.status_code == 400
    assert json_data['error'] == 'Bad Request'
```

This test checks the behavior when required data is missing from the request.

2. Test Retrieving Non-Existent Item:

```python
def test_get_non_existent_item(client):
    response = client.get('/item/999')
    assert response.status_code == 404
```

This test verifies that a request for a non-existent item returns a 404 status code.

3. Test Updating Non-Existent Item:

```python
def test_update_non_existent_item(client):
    response = client.put('/item/999', json={'name': 'Apple', 'price': 1.5})
    assert response.status_code == 404
```

This test ensures that updating a non-existent item returns a 404 status code.

Using Mocking for External Dependencies

If your Flask application interacts with external services, use mocking to simulate these interactions during testing. For instance, using the `unittest.mock` library:

```python
from unittest.mock import patch

@patch('app.external_service_call')
def test_external_service_call(mock_service, client):
```

```
    mock_service.return_value = {'response': 'success'}
    response = client.get('/external-service')
    json_data = response.get_json()
    assert response.status_code == 200
    assert json_data['response'] == 'success'
```

Test Coverage

To measure test coverage, use `pytest-cov`. Install it via pip:

```bash
pip install pytest-cov
```

Run tests with coverage reporting:

```bash
pytest --cov=app tests/
```

This command provides a report showing which parts of your code are covered by tests and highlights areas that need additional testing.

Continuous Integration (CI)

Integrating testing into your CI pipeline ensures tests run automatically on code changes, helping catch issues early. Here's an example using GitHub Actions:

Create a `.github/workflows/test.yml` file:

```yaml
name: Flask API Tests

on: [push, pull_request]

jobs:
  test:
    runs-on: ubuntu-latest

    steps:
    - uses: actions/checkout@v2

    - name: Set up Python
      uses: actions/setup-python@v2
      with:
        python-version: '3.8'

    - name: Install dependencies
      run: |
        python -m pip install --upgrade pip
```

```
    pip install Flask pytest pytest-flask pytest-cov flask_sqlalchemy

  - name: Run tests
    run: |
      pytest --cov=app tests/
```

Setting up a comprehensive testing environment for Flask applications is vital for ensuring the reliability and correctness of your API, particularly in mobile app development where consistent and accurate data exchange is critical. By following the practices and examples outlined above, you can establish a robust testing suite that covers Flask routes, views, and database interactions. This approach not only enhances code quality and maintainability but also provides confidence in the stability of your application as it evolves. Integrating these tests into a CI pipeline further ensures that your application remains stable and reliable through continuous development and deployment.

Writing Clean and Maintainable Code with Unit Tests for a Flask API in Mobile App Development

In modern software development, writing clean and maintainable code is crucial, particularly when developing APIs for mobile applications. Unit tests are indispensable in ensuring code quality, reliability, and maintainability. This guide explores best practices for writing clean and maintainable code, focusing on a Flask API tailored for mobile app development, with comprehensive examples of unit tests.

Clean and Maintainable Code

Clean and maintainable code is readable, well-structured, and easy to understand. Such code enhances collaboration, reduces bugs, and simplifies debugging and maintenance.

Key Principles

1. Readability: Code should be easily understood by others.

2. Simplicity: Avoid unnecessary complexity.

3. Modularity: Break down large functions into smaller, reusable functions.

4. Consistency: Follow consistent coding styles and conventions.

5. Documentation: Document code and APIs clearly.

Example: Flask API

Consider a simple Flask API for managing a list of tasks in a to-do application. This example demonstrates clean and maintainable code practices.

Directory Structure

```
```
flask_api/
├── app/
│   ├── __init__.py
│   ├── models.py
│   ├── routes.py
│   ├── services.py
│   └── tests/
│   ├── __init__.py
│   └── test_routes.py
│
├── config.py
├── run.py
```
```

└── requirements.txt
```

### `run.py`

This file initializes the Flask application.

```python
from app import create_app

app = create_app()

if __name__ == "__main__":
    app.run(debug=True)
```

`app/__init__.py`

This file sets up the Flask app and registers the blueprints.

```python
from flask import Flask
from .routes import main

def create_app():
    app = Flask(__name__)

```
    app.config.from_object('config.Config')

    app.register_blueprint(main)

    return app
```

`app/models.py`

This file defines the data models.

```python
from flask_sqlalchemy import SQLAlchemy

db = SQLAlchemy()

class Task(db.Model):
    id = db.Column(db.Integer, primary_key=True)
    title = db.Column(db.String(100), nullable=False)
    description = db.Column(db.String(200), nullable=True)
    completed = db.Column(db.Boolean, default=False)
```

`app/routes.py`

This file defines the routes for the API.

```python
from flask import Blueprint, request, jsonify
from .models import db, Task

main = Blueprint('main', __name__)

@main.route('/tasks', methods=['GET'])
def get_tasks():
    tasks = Task.query.all()
    return jsonify([task.to_dict() for task in tasks])

@main.route('/tasks', methods=['POST'])
def add_task():
    data = request.get_json()
    new_task = Task(
        title=data['title'],
        description=data.get('description'),
        completed=data.get('completed', False)
    )
    db.session.add(new_task)
    db.session.commit()
    return jsonify(new_task.to_dict()), 201

@main.route('/tasks/<int:task_id>', methods=['PUT'])
def update_task(task_id):
    task = Task.query.get_or_404(task_id)
```

```
    data = request.get_json()
    task.title = data.get('title', task.title)
    task.description = data.get('description',
task.description)
    task.completed = data.get('completed', task.completed)
    db.session.commit()
    return jsonify(task.to_dict())

@main.route('/tasks/<int:task_id>',
methods=['DELETE'])
def delete_task(task_id):
    task = Task.query.get_or_404(task_id)
    db.session.delete(task)
    db.session.commit()
    return '', 204
```

`app/services.py`

This file contains reusable service functions.

```python
from .models import db, Task

def get_all_tasks():
    return Task.query.all()
```

```
def create_task(title, description, completed=False):
    new_task = Task(
        title=title,
        description=description,
        completed=completed
    )
    db.session.add(new_task)
    db.session.commit()
    return new_task

def update_task(task, data):
    task.title = data.get('title', task.title)
    task.description = data.get('description', task.description)
    task.completed = data.get('completed', task.completed)
    db.session.commit()
    return task

def delete_task(task):
    db.session.delete(task)
    db.session.commit()
```

Unit Tests

Unit tests validate the functionality of individual units of code. For Flask APIs, this often involves testing routes, models, and services.

Setup Testing Environment

Add necessary testing packages to `requirements.txt`.

```
Flask
Flask-SQLAlchemy
pytest
pytest-flask
```

Create a `tests` folder with an `__init__.py` file to make it a package.

`tests/test_routes.py`

This file tests the API routes.

```python
import pytest
from app import create_app, db
from app.models import Task
```

```python
@pytest.fixture
def client():
    app = create_app()
    app.config['TESTING'] = True
    app.config['SQLALCHEMY_DATABASE_URI'] = 'sqlite:///:memory:'

    with app.test_client() as client:
        with app.app_context():
            db.create_all()
            yield client
            db.drop_all()

def test_get_tasks(client):
    response = client.get('/tasks')
    assert response.status_code == 200
    assert response.json == []

def test_add_task(client):
    response = client.post('/tasks', json={
        'title': 'New Task',
        'description': 'Task Description',
        'completed': False
    })
    assert response.status_code == 201
    assert response.json['title'] == 'New Task'
```

```python
def test_update_task(client):
    # First, add a task
    response = client.post('/tasks', json={
        'title': 'Task to Update',
        'description': 'Update Description',
        'completed': False
    })
    task_id = response.json['id']

    # Now, update the task
    response = client.put(f'/tasks/{task_id}', json={
        'title': 'Updated Task',
        'completed': True
    })
    assert response.status_code == 200
    assert response.json['title'] == 'Updated Task'
    assert response.json['completed'] is True

def test_delete_task(client):
    # First, add a task
    response = client.post('/tasks', json={
        'title': 'Task to Delete',
        'description': 'Delete Description',
        'completed': False
    })
    task_id = response.json['id']
```

```
    # Now, delete the task
    response = client.delete(f'/tasks/{task_id}')
    assert response.status_code == 204
```

Running Tests

To run the tests, use the following command:

```sh
pytest
```

Best Practices

1. Test Coverage: Aim for high test coverage. Test all critical paths and edge cases.

2. Isolation: Tests should be isolated and independent. Avoid dependencies on external systems.

3. Descriptive Test Names: Use descriptive names for test functions to convey their purpose.

4. Setup and Teardown: Use fixtures for setup and teardown to ensure a clean test environment.

Advanced Testing

For more comprehensive testing, consider adding tests for:

- **Error Handling:** Verify that the API correctly handles and returns appropriate error messages.

- **Edge Cases:** Test edge cases, such as empty inputs, very large inputs, and invalid data.

- **Performance**: Measure and ensure that the API meets performance requirements.

Writing clean and maintainable code is fundamental for the success of any software project. This is particularly important in mobile app development, where the backend API must be robust and reliable. By adhering to clean coding principles and implementing thorough unit tests, you can ensure that your Flask API is well-structured, maintainable, and dependable. This guide provides a solid foundation, but continuous learning and adaptation are key to mastering these practices.

Chapter 6

Choosing a Deployment Strategy: On-premise vs. Cloud Options for Flask APIs in Mobile App Development

Deploying a Flask API for mobile app development requires careful consideration of various factors, including scalability, security, cost, and maintenance. This guide explores the two main deployment options: on-premise and cloud-based solutions. We'll delve into the advantages, disadvantages, and implementation details of each approach, accompanied by code examples tailored for Flask APIs.

On-premise Deployment

On-premise deployment involves hosting the Flask API on servers physically located within the organization's premises.

Advantages

1. Control: Complete control over hardware, software, and infrastructure.

2. Data Security: Direct control over data security measures.

3. Compliance: Easier compliance with regulatory requirements.

Disadvantages

1. Infrastructure Costs: High upfront costs for hardware, networking, and maintenance.

2. Scalability: Limited scalability, requiring additional hardware procurement and setup.

3. Maintenance Overhead: Responsibility for system updates, patches, and backups.

Implementation

Hardware Setup

Procure servers meeting the requirements for hosting the Flask API. Install and configure necessary software components such as Python, Flask, and database servers.

Networking

Set up networking infrastructure, including routers, switches, firewalls, and load balancers, to ensure proper communication between the Flask API and client devices.

Security Measures

Implement security measures such as firewalls, intrusion detection systems, and encryption protocols to safeguard data and prevent unauthorized access.

Maintenance Plan

Establish a maintenance plan for regular updates, patches, backups, and disaster recovery procedures.

Cloud Deployment

Cloud deployment involves hosting the Flask API on cloud-based platforms such as Amazon Web Services (AWS), Google Cloud Platform (GCP), or Microsoft Azure.

Advantages

1. Scalability: Easy scalability with on-demand resources and auto-scaling features.

2. Cost Efficiency: Pay-as-you-go pricing model, eliminating upfront hardware costs.

3. Managed Services: Access to managed services for databases, storage, and networking.

4. Global Reach: Ability to deploy resources in multiple regions for better latency and availability.

Disadvantages

1. Dependency on Providers: Reliance on cloud service providers for uptime and service availability.

2. Data Security Concerns: Potential security risks associated with cloud storage and transmission.

3. Vendor Lock-in: Difficulty in migrating away from a specific cloud provider once deeply integrated.

Implementation

Cloud Provider Selection

Choose a cloud provider based on factors such as pricing, services offered, reliability, and compliance with regulatory requirements.

Resource Provisioning

Provision virtual machines or container instances to host the Flask API. Utilize managed services like AWS Elastic Beanstalk or Google App Engine for easier deployment and management.

Networking Configuration

Configure networking settings, including virtual private clouds (VPCs), subnets, security groups, and load balancers, to ensure secure communication and high availability.

Security Measures

Implement security best practices, such as encryption at rest and in transit, identity and access management (IAM), and network security groups, to protect data and prevent unauthorized access.

Code Examples

On-premise Deployment

```python
# Flask API code
from flask import Flask

app = Flask(__name__)

@app.route('/')
def hello():
    return 'Hello, World!'

if __name__ == '__main__':
    app.run(host='0.0.0.0', port=5000)
```

Cloud Deployment (AWS Elastic Beanstalk)

```python
# Flask API code
from flask import Flask

app = Flask(__name__)

@app.route('/')
def hello():
    return 'Hello, World!'
```

```
if __name__ == '__main__':
    app.run(debug=True)
```

`Dockerfile`

```Dockerfile
FROM python:3.9-slim

WORKDIR /app

COPY requirements.txt .

RUN pip install --no-cache-dir -r requirements.txt

COPY . .

CMD ["python", "app.py"]
```

`requirements.txt`

```
Flask==2.0.1
```

Choosing the right deployment strategy for a Flask API in mobile app development depends on various factors, including budget, scalability requirements, data security concerns, and regulatory compliance. On-premise deployment offers control and security but comes with higher upfront costs and maintenance overhead. In contrast, cloud deployment provides scalability, cost efficiency, and managed services but entails dependency on cloud providers and potential security risks. Ultimately, the decision should align with the organization's goals, resources, and technical expertise. By understanding the advantages, disadvantages, and implementation details of each approach, developers can make informed decisions to ensure the successful deployment and operation of Flask APIs for mobile app development.

Deploying Your Flask API to Production Environments

Deploying a Flask API to production environments is a crucial step in the development process of mobile applications. Production deployment ensures that your API is accessible to users securely, reliably, and with optimal performance. In this guide, we'll explore the steps involved in deploying a Flask API to production environments, covering considerations, best practices, and code examples tailored for mobile app development.

Considerations Before Deployment

Before deploying your Flask API to production, consider the following:

1. Environment Configuration: Define environment-specific configurations for production, including database connection strings, API keys, and security settings.

2. Security: Implement security measures such as HTTPS, authentication, and authorization to protect sensitive data and prevent unauthorized access.

3. Scalability: Design your deployment architecture to scale horizontally to handle increasing traffic and workload demands.

4. Monitoring and Logging: Set up monitoring and logging mechanisms to track performance, detect errors, and troubleshoot issues effectively.

5. Backup and Recovery: Establish backup and recovery procedures to ensure data integrity and minimize downtime in case of failures.

Production Deployment Options

There are several deployment options for Flask APIs in production environments, including traditional servers, containerized solutions, and serverless architectures. Let's explore two popular approaches: deploying to virtual machines (VMs) and containerized deployment using Docker and Kubernetes.

Deploying to Virtual Machines (VMs)

Deploying to VMs involves provisioning virtual servers and deploying the Flask API directly onto these instances.

Steps:

1. Provision VMs: Set up virtual machines on your chosen cloud provider (e.g., AWS EC2, Google Compute Engine).

2. Install Dependencies: Install Python, Flask, and any necessary libraries on the VMs.

3. Deploy Flask API: Upload your Flask API code to the VMs and configure the web server (e.g., Nginx, Apache) to serve the API.

4. Configure DNS: Map your domain name to the public IP address of the VMs for easy access.

Containerized Deployment with Docker and Kubernetes

Containerized deployment offers a more lightweight and scalable solution using Docker containers orchestrated by Kubernetes.

Steps:

1. Containerize Flask API: Create a Docker image containing your Flask API code, dependencies, and runtime environment.

2. Push Image to Registry: Push the Docker image to a container registry like Docker Hub, AWS ECR, or Google Container Registry.

3. Provision Kubernetes Cluster: Set up a Kubernetes cluster on your preferred cloud provider or on-premise environment.

4. Deploy with Kubernetes: Define Kubernetes manifests (e.g., Deployment, Service) to deploy and manage the Flask API containers within the cluster.

Code Examples

Dockerfile

```Dockerfile
FROM python:3.9-slim

WORKDIR /app

COPY requirements.txt .

RUN pip install --no-cache-dir -r requirements.txt

COPY . .

CMD ["gunicorn", "--bind", "0.0.0.0:5000", "app:app"]
```

Kubernetes Deployment Manifest (deployment.yaml)

```yaml
apiVersion: apps/v1
kind: Deployment
```

```yaml
metadata:
  name: flask-api-deployment
spec:
  replicas: 3
  selector:
    matchLabels:
      app: flask-api
  template:
    metadata:
      labels:
        app: flask-api
    spec:
      containers:
      - name: flask-api
        image: yourregistry/flask-api:latest
        ports:
        - containerPort: 5000
---
apiVersion: v1
kind: Service
metadata:
  name: flask-api-service
spec:
  selector:
    app: flask-api
  ports:
    - protocol: TCP
```

```
    port: 80
    targetPort: 5000
 type: LoadBalancer
```

Best Practices

1. Immutable Infrastructure: Treat infrastructure as code and use version-controlled configurations for reproducibility and consistency.

2. Health Checks: Implement health checks to monitor the status of your Flask API and ensure high availability.

3. Secret Management: Store sensitive information such as API keys and database credentials securely using environment variables or a dedicated secrets management service.

4. Continuous Deployment: Automate deployment pipelines with CI/CD tools like Jenkins, GitLab CI, or GitHub Actions to streamline the deployment process.

5. Rolling Updates: Use rolling updates and blue-green deployments to minimize downtime and maintain service availability during updates.

Deploying your Flask API to production environments requires careful planning, consideration of various factors, and adherence to best practices. Whether deploying to virtual machines or utilizing containerized solutions with Docker and Kubernetes, it's essential to prioritize security, scalability, reliability, and automation. By following the steps outlined in this guide and leveraging code examples, you can deploy your Flask API confidently, ensuring optimal performance and availability for your mobile applications.

Scalability Considerations for High Traffic Mobile Apps

Scalability is a critical aspect of developing mobile apps, especially as they grow in popularity and user base. Ensuring that your Flask API can handle high traffic is essential for maintaining a seamless user experience. In this guide, we'll explore scalability considerations for high traffic mobile apps, including architectural decisions, database optimization, caching strategies, and code examples tailored for Flask APIs.

Understanding Scalability

Scalability refers to the ability of a system to handle increasing workload without compromising performance or reliability. In the context of mobile apps, scalability ensures that the backend infrastructure can accommodate a growing number of users and requests without experiencing downtime or degradation in response times.

Scalability Considerations

1. Load Balancing

Load balancing distributes incoming traffic across multiple servers to ensure optimal resource utilization and prevent overload on any single server.

Example:

```python
# Load Balancing with Flask
from flask import Flask
from flask.views import MethodView

app = Flask(__name__)

class MyView(MethodView):
    def get(self):
        return "Hello, World!"

app.add_url_rule('/',
view_func=MyView.as_view('my_view'))
```

```
if __name__ == '__main__':
    app.run(host='0.0.0.0', port=5000)
```

2. Horizontal Scaling

Horizontal scaling involves adding more servers or instances to handle increased traffic. This can be achieved by deploying multiple instances of your Flask API across different machines or using container orchestration tools like Kubernetes.

Example:

```yaml
# Kubernetes Deployment Manifest (horizontal scaling)
apiVersion: apps/v1
kind: Deployment
metadata:
  name: flask-api-deployment
spec:
  replicas: 3
  selector:
    matchLabels:
      app: flask-api
  template:
```

```
  metadata:
    labels:
      app: flask-api
  spec:
    containers:
    - name: flask-api
      image: yourregistry/flask-api:latest
      ports:
      - containerPort: 5000
```

3. Database Optimization

Optimizing database queries and schema design can significantly improve the performance of your Flask API, especially under high load. Consider using indexes, denormalization, and database sharding to distribute the workload evenly across multiple database servers.

Example:

```python
# Database Optimization with SQLAlchemy
from flask import Flask
from flask_sqlalchemy import SQLAlchemy

app = Flask(__name__)
```

```python
app.config['SQLALCHEMY_DATABASE_URI'] = 'sqlite:///app.db'
db = SQLAlchemy(app)

class User(db.Model):
    id = db.Column(db.Integer, primary_key=True)
    username = db.Column(db.String(50), unique=True, nullable=False)

    def __repr__(self):
        return '<User %r>' % self.username

@app.route('/')
def hello():
    users = User.query.all()
    return 'Hello, World!'

if __name__ == '__main__':
    app.run(host='0.0.0.0', port=5000)
```

4. Caching

Implementing caching mechanisms can reduce the load on your Flask API by serving frequently accessed data from memory or a dedicated caching server. Consider using tools like Redis or Memcached for caching commonly requested data.

Example:

```python
# Caching with Flask-Cache
from flask import Flask
from flask_cache import Cache

app = Flask(__name__)
cache = Cache(app, config={'CACHE_TYPE': 'simple'})

@cache.cached(timeout=60)
@app.route('/')
def hello():
    return 'Hello, World!'

if __name__ == '__main__':
    app.run(host='0.0.0.0', port=5000)
```

5. Asynchronous Processing

Using asynchronous processing techniques such as Celery with Redis or RabbitMQ can offload time-consuming tasks from the main Flask API process, improving responsiveness and scalability.

Example:

```python
# Asynchronous Processing with Celery
from flask import Flask
from celery import Celery

app = Flask(__name__)
celery = Celery(app)

@celery.task
def long_running_task():
    # Perform time-consuming task here
    pass

@app.route('/')
def hello():
    long_running_task.delay()
    return 'Hello, World!'

if __name__ == '__main__':
    app.run(host='0.0.0.0', port=5000)
```

Best Practices

1. Monitor Performance: Regularly monitor the performance of your Flask API using tools like Prometheus, Grafana, or New Relic to identify bottlenecks and areas for improvement.

2. Auto-scaling: Set up auto-scaling policies to automatically provision or terminate instances based on predefined metrics such as CPU utilization or request latency.

3. Fault Tolerance: Design your architecture to be resilient to failures by implementing redundancy, failover mechanisms, and graceful degradation.

4. Testing: Conduct performance testing and load testing to simulate high traffic scenarios and validate the scalability of your Flask API.

5. Continuous Optimization: Continuously optimize your Flask API based on usage patterns, feedback, and performance metrics to ensure optimal scalability and responsiveness.

Scalability is a fundamental aspect of building high traffic mobile apps with Flask APIs. By considering load balancing, horizontal scaling, database optimization, caching strategies, and asynchronous processing, you can design a scalable backend infrastructure that can handle increasing workload with ease. Implementing best practices and monitoring tools ensures that your Flask API remains responsive, reliable, and performant, even under heavy traffic conditions.

Monitoring and Maintaining Your Deployed Flask API

Monitoring and maintaining a deployed Flask API is essential to ensure its reliability, performance, and security. By continuously monitoring key metrics and performing regular maintenance tasks, you can proactively identify issues, optimize performance, and ensure a seamless user experience for your mobile app. In this guide, we'll explore monitoring tools, important metrics to track, maintenance tasks, and code examples tailored for Flask APIs in mobile app development.

Monitoring Tools

Several monitoring tools are available for tracking the health and performance of your deployed Flask API. Some popular options include:

1. Prometheus: A powerful open-source monitoring and alerting toolkit designed for reliability and scalability.

2. Grafana: An open-source analytics and monitoring platform that integrates seamlessly with Prometheus and other data sources.

3. New Relic: A cloud-based observability platform that provides real-time insights into your application's performance and user experience.

4. ELK Stack (Elasticsearch, Logstash, Kibana): A combination of open-source tools for centralized logging, log analysis, and visualization.

Important Metrics to Track

When monitoring your deployed Flask API, it's essential to track key metrics that provide insights into its health, performance, and usage. Some important metrics to track include:

1. Response Time: The time taken to process and respond to incoming requests. High response times can indicate performance issues or bottlenecks.

2. Error Rate: The percentage of requests that result in errors or failures. Monitoring error rates helps identify issues that need immediate attention.

3. Request Rate: The number of requests received by the Flask API per unit of time. Tracking request rates helps anticipate traffic spikes and scale resources accordingly.

4. CPU and Memory Usage: The utilization of CPU and memory resources on the server hosting the Flask API. Monitoring resource usage helps identify resource constraints and plan for scalability.

5. Database Performance: Metrics such as query latency, throughput, and connection pool usage for databases accessed by the Flask API. Monitoring database performance ensures optimal data access and query execution.

Maintenance Tasks

In addition to monitoring, performing regular maintenance tasks is essential to ensure the continued health and performance of your deployed Flask API. Some important maintenance tasks include:

1. Software Updates: Regularly update dependencies, libraries, and frameworks used by your Flask API to patch security vulnerabilities and access new features and optimizations.

2. Database Maintenance: Perform routine database maintenance tasks such as vacuuming, indexing, and optimizing queries to ensure optimal database performance and data integrity.

3. Log Management: Configure logging to capture relevant information, errors, and exceptions generated by your Flask API. Regularly review and analyze logs to identify issues and trends.

4. Backup and Disaster Recovery: Implement backup and disaster recovery procedures to protect against data loss and ensure business continuity in case of failures or disasters.

5. Security Audits: Conduct periodic security audits to identify and address potential vulnerabilities in your Flask API, including security misconfigurations, outdated dependencies, and unauthorized access.

Code Examples

Logging Configuration

```python
# Logging Configuration in Flask
import logging
from flask import Flask

app = Flask(__name__)

# Configure logging
logging.basicConfig(filename='flask_api.log', level=logging.INFO)

@app.route('/')
def hello():
    app.logger.info('Request received for /')
    return 'Hello, World!'

if __name__ == '__main__':
    app.run(host='0.0.0.0', port=5000)
```

Database Maintenance with SQLAlchemy

```python
# Database Maintenance with SQLAlchemy
from flask import Flask
```

```python
from flask_sqlalchemy import SQLAlchemy

app = Flask(__name__)
app.config['SQLALCHEMY_DATABASE_URI'] = 'sqlite:///app.db'
db = SQLAlchemy(app)

class User(db.Model):
    id = db.Column(db.Integer, primary_key=True)
    username = db.Column(db.String(50), unique=True, nullable=False)

    def __repr__(self):
        return '<User %r>' % self.username

# Indexing example
db.Index('idx_username', User.username)

if __name__ == '__main__':
    app.run(host='0.0.0.0', port=5000)
```

Performance Monitoring with Prometheus

```python
# Performance Monitoring with Prometheus
from flask import Flask
```

```
from prometheus_flask_exporter import PrometheusMetrics

app = Flask(__name__)
metrics = PrometheusMetrics(app)

@app.route('/')
def hello():
    return 'Hello, World!'

if __name__ == '__main__':
    app.run(host='0.0.0.0', port=5000)
```

Best Practices

1. Proactive Monitoring: Monitor your Flask API proactively to detect issues before they impact users and take appropriate actions to mitigate them.

2. Alerting: Set up alerting mechanisms to notify you of critical issues, anomalies, or performance degradation in real-time.

3. Continuous Improvement: Continuously analyze monitoring data, identify areas for improvement, and iterate on your Flask API to optimize performance and reliability.

4. Documentation: Document monitoring configurations, maintenance procedures, and troubleshooting steps to facilitate collaboration and knowledge sharing among team members.

5. Scalability Planning: Plan for scalability from the outset and monitor scalability metrics to ensure that your Flask API can handle increasing traffic and workload demands.

Monitoring and maintaining your deployed Flask API is crucial for ensuring its reliability, performance, and security in production environments. By leveraging monitoring tools, tracking key metrics, performing regular maintenance tasks, and following best practices, you can proactively identify and address issues, optimize performance, and provide a seamless user experience for your mobile app users. Incorporate monitoring and maintenance into your development process to build robust and resilient Flask APIs that meet the demands of high traffic mobile apps.

Chapter 7

Flask in Action - Inspiring Examples of Mobile Apps

Building a Social Media App Backend with Flask

Creating a social media app backend with Flask can be an exciting project. Flask is a lightweight and flexible micro-framework for Python, making it a great choice for building RESTful APIs to power mobile app development. In this tutorial, we'll cover the steps to build a basic social media backend using Flask.

Setting Up Flask:

First, make sure you have Python and pip installed on your system. Then, create a new directory for your project and navigate into it:

```bash
mkdir social_media_backend
cd social_media_backend
```

Next, create a virtual environment to isolate your project dependencies:

```bash
python3 -m venv venv
```

Activate the virtual environment:

```bash
source venv/bin/activate
```

Now, install Flask:

```bash
pip install Flask
```

Creating the Flask App:

Create a new Python file named `app.py` in your project directory. This file will contain the code for our Flask application.

```python
from flask import Flask, jsonify, request

app = Flask(__name__)
```

```python
# Dummy data for testing
posts = [
    {'id': 1, 'title': 'First Post', 'content': 'Hello, world!', 'author': 'Alice'},
    {'id': 2, 'title': 'Second Post', 'content': 'Flask is awesome!', 'author': 'Bob'}
]

# Endpoint to get all posts
@app.route('/posts', methods=['GET'])
def get_posts():
    return jsonify(posts)

# Endpoint to create a new post
@app.route('/posts', methods=['POST'])
def create_post():
    data = request.json
    new_post = {
        'id': len(posts) + 1,
        'title': data['title'],
        'content': data['content'],
        'author': data['author']
    }
    posts.append(new_post)
    return jsonify(new_post), 201

if __name__ == '__main__':
```

```
    app.run(debug=True)
```

This is a basic Flask application with two endpoints: one to get all posts and another to create a new post. We're using dummy data for testing, but in a real-world scenario, you'd likely interact with a database.

Testing the Endpoints:

Start the Flask development server by running:

```bash
python app.py
```

Now, you can test the endpoints using tools like cURL or Postman. For example, to get all posts:

```bash
curl http://127.0.0.1:5000/posts
```

To create a new post:

```bash
```

```
curl -X POST -H "Content-Type: application/json" -d
'{"title":"New Post", "content":"This is a new post.",
"author":"Charlie"}' http://127.0.0.1:5000/posts
```

Adding More Functionality:

You can extend this basic backend to include features like user authentication, likes, comments, and more. Here's an example of adding comments to posts:

```python
# Dummy data for testing
comments = [
    {'id': 1, 'post_id': 1, 'content': 'Great post!', 'author': 'David'},
    {'id': 2, 'post_id': 1, 'content': 'Thanks!', 'author': 'Alice'}
]

# Endpoint to get comments for a specific post
@app.route('/posts/<int:post_id>/comments', methods=['GET'])
def get_comments(post_id):
    post_comments = [comment for comment in comments if comment['post_id'] == post_id]
    return jsonify(post_comments)
```

```
# Endpoint to add a comment to a post
@app.route('/posts/<int:post_id>/comments',
methods=['POST'])
def add_comment(post_id):
    data = request.json
    new_comment = {
        'id': len(comments) + 1,
        'post_id': post_id,
        'content': data['content'],
        'author': data['author']
    }
    comments.append(new_comment)
    return jsonify(new_comment), 201
```
```

In this tutorial, we've covered the basics of building a social media backend with Flask. We've created endpoints for retrieving posts, creating posts, retrieving comments for a post, and adding comments to a post. Flask provides a simple and flexible framework for building powerful RESTful APIs to support your mobile app development needs. Remember, this is just a starting point, and you can extend and customize your backend to meet the specific requirements of your social media app.
```

Crafting a Location-Based Service with Flask and Geolocation

Crafting a location-based service with Flask and geolocation capabilities can greatly enhance the functionality of your mobile app. In this tutorial, we'll explore how to build such a service using Flask and integrate geolocation features to provide location-specific information.

Setting Up Flask and Geolocation:

Before we start, make sure you have Python and pip installed on your system. Create a new directory for your project and navigate into it:

```bash
mkdir location_service
cd location_service
```

Create a virtual environment to isolate your project dependencies:

```bash
python3 -m venv venv
```

Activate the virtual environment:

```bash
source venv/bin/activate
```

Install Flask and the Flask-RESTful extension:

```bash
pip install Flask Flask-RESTful
```

We'll also need a geolocation service provider. For this tutorial, we'll use the free service provided by the OpenStreetMap Nominatim API. You can sign up for an API key if you plan to use this service in production.

Creating the Flask App:

Create a new Python file named `app.py` in your project directory. This file will contain the code for our Flask application.

```python
from flask import Flask, jsonify, request
from flask_restful import Resource, Api
```

```python
import requests

app = Flask(__name__)
api = Api(app)

# Geolocation API endpoint
GEOCODE_URL = 'https://nominatim.openstreetmap.org/reverse'

# Endpoint to get location information
class Location(Resource):
    def get(self):
        # Get latitude and longitude from request parameters
        lat = request.args.get('lat')
        lon = request.args.get('lon')

        # Make a request to the geolocation API
        params = {'lat': lat, 'lon': lon, 'format': 'json'}
        response = requests.get(GEOCODE_URL, params=params)

        # Parse the response and extract location information
        if response.status_code == 200:
            data = response.json()
            location_info = {
```

```
            'address': data.get('display_name', 'Location not found'),
            'latitude': lat,
            'longitude': lon
        }
        return jsonify(location_info)
    else:
        return jsonify({'error': 'Failed to retrieve location information'}), 500

api.add_resource(Location, '/location')

if __name__ == '__main__':
    app.run(debug=True)
```

Explaining the Code:

We've created a Flask application with a single endpoint `/location` that accepts latitude and longitude coordinates as query parameters. It then makes a request to the OpenStreetMap Nominatim API to reverse geocode these coordinates and retrieve location information.

Testing the Endpoint:

Start the Flask development server by running:

```bash
python app.py
```

Now, you can test the endpoint using tools like cURL or Postman. For example:

```bash
curl http://127.0.0.1:5000/location?lat=51.5074&lon=0.1278
```

This will return location information for the coordinates of London, UK.

Enhancing the Service:

You can extend this location-based service to include additional features such as:

1. Search by Location Name: Allow users to search for location information by name using the Nominatim search API.

2. Nearby Places: Provide information about nearby places such as restaurants, hotels, or landmarks based on the user's current location.

3. User Authentication: Implement user authentication to personalize the service and store user preferences or favorite locations.

4. Geofencing: Define virtual boundaries and trigger actions when a user enters or exits a specific geographical area.

In this tutorial, we've explored how to create a location-based service with Flask and geolocation capabilities. By integrating with the OpenStreetMap Nominatim API, we can retrieve location information based on latitude and longitude coordinates. With additional features and enhancements, you can tailor this service to meet the specific needs of your mobile app and provide valuable location-based experiences to your users.

Designing a Real-Time Chat Application with Flask APIs

Designing a real-time chat application with Flask APIs can be an exciting project. In this tutorial, we'll cover the steps to build a basic real-time chat application using

Flask for the backend API and WebSocket technology for real-time communication. Let's dive in!

Setting Up Flask and WebSocket:

First, make sure you have Python and pip installed on your system. Create a new directory for your project and navigate into it:

```bash
mkdir chat_app
cd chat_app
```

Create a virtual environment to isolate your project dependencies:

```bash
python3 -m venv venv
```

Activate the virtual environment:

```bash
source venv/bin/activate
```

Install Flask and the Flask-SocketIO extension for WebSocket support:

```bash
pip install Flask Flask-SocketIO
```

Creating the Flask App:

Create a new Python file named `app.py` in your project directory. This file will contain the code for our Flask application.

```python
from flask import Flask, render_template
from flask_socketio import SocketIO

app = Flask(__name__)
socketio = SocketIO(app)

# Route to serve the HTML file
@app.route('/')
def index():
    return render_template('index.html')

# WebSocket event handler for new messages
@socketio.on('message')
```

```
def handle_message(message):
    print('Received message: ' + message)
    # Broadcast the message to all connected clients
    socketio.emit('message', message)

if __name__ == '__main__':
    socketio.run(app)
```

Creating the HTML Template:

Create a new directory named `templates` in your project directory, and inside it, create a new HTML file named `index.html`. This file will contain the frontend code for our chat application.

```html
<!DOCTYPE html>
<html lang="en">
<head>
    <meta charset="UTF-8">
    <meta name="viewport" content="width=device-width, initial-scale=1.0">
    <title>Real-Time Chat App</title>
    <script src="https://cdnjs.cloudflare.com/ajax/libs/socket.io/4.0.1/socket.io.js" integrity="sha512-
```

```
EExHH0Gp3YF6GD/98XGwB9YCEmFiG7cnnYOu0r8
6ESRnIiSX7R2h/oPaxr6ScFMC6r/jARxybh5JW3NtWg
szQQ==" crossorigin="anonymous"></script>
</head>
<body>
  <h1>Real-Time Chat App</h1>
  <ul id="messages"></ul>
  <input id="message_input" autocomplete="off"
/><button onclick="sendMessage()">Send</button>

  <script>
    var socket = io();

    // Function to send a message
    function sendMessage() {
       var message = document.getElementById('message_input').value;
       socket.emit('message', message);

document.getElementById('message_input').value = '';
    }

    // Function to handle incoming messages
    socket.on('message', function(message) {
       var li = document.createElement('li');
       li.textContent = message;
```

```
    document.getElementById('messages').appendChild(li);
  });
</script>
</body>
</html>
```

Explaining the Code:

We've created a Flask application with a route to serve the HTML file containing our chat interface. We've also set up a WebSocket event handler to receive and broadcast messages to all connected clients. The HTML template contains JavaScript code to establish a WebSocket connection and handle sending and displaying messages.

Testing the Chat Application:

Start the Flask development server by running:

```bash
python app.py
```

Now, open your web browser and navigate to `http://127.0.0.1:5000`. You should see the chat interface. Open multiple browser tabs or windows to simulate different users and start sending messages. You'll notice that messages are instantly displayed in real-time to all connected clients.

Enhancing the Chat Application:

You can enhance this basic chat application in several ways, such as:

1. User Authentication: Implement user authentication to identify and personalize user interactions.

2. Message Persistence: Store chat messages in a database to maintain chat history across server restarts.

3. Private Messaging: Allow users to send private messages to specific recipients.

4. Emojis and Multimedia: Support emojis, file attachments, and multimedia messages for richer communication.

5. User Status: Display online/offline status for users and indicate when users are typing.

In this tutorial, we've explored how to design a real-time chat application using Flask for the backend API and WebSocket technology for real-time communication. By following these steps and enhancing the application with additional features, you can build a robust and interactive chat platform for various use cases, including team collaboration, customer support, or social networking.

Exploring Additional Mobile App Use Cases with Flask

Exploring additional mobile app use cases with Flask can open up a world of possibilities for developers. Flask's flexibility and simplicity make it a great choice for building APIs to power various mobile app functionalities. In this tutorial, we'll explore some additional use cases and demonstrate how to implement them using Flask APIs.

Use Case 1: User Authentication

User authentication is a crucial feature for many mobile apps to ensure user privacy and security. Flask provides several libraries and tools to implement authentication, such as Flask-Login and JSON Web Tokens (JWT).

```python
from flask import Flask, jsonify, request
from flask_login import LoginManager, UserMixin, login_user, logout_user, login_required

app = Flask(__name__)
app.secret_key = 'your_secret_key'
login_manager = LoginManager()
login_manager.init_app(app)

# Dummy user database
class User(UserMixin):
    def __init__(self, id):
        self.id = id

users = {
    1: User(1),
    2: User(2)
}

# User loader function for Flask-Login
@login_manager.user_loader
def load_user(user_id):
    return users.get(int(user_id))

# Login endpoint
@app.route('/login', methods=['POST'])
```

```
def login():
    data = request.json
    user_id = data.get('user_id')
    if user_id and int(user_id) in users:
        user = users[int(user_id)]
        login_user(user)
        return jsonify({'message': 'Login successful'})
    else:
        return jsonify({'message': 'Invalid user ID'}), 401

# Logout endpoint
@app.route('/logout')
@login_required
def logout():
    logout_user()
    return jsonify({'message': 'Logout successful'})

# Protected endpoint
@app.route('/protected')
@login_required
def protected():
    return jsonify({'message': 'You are authenticated'})

if __name__ == '__main__':
    app.run(debug=True)
```
```
```

Use Case 2: Push Notifications

Push notifications are a powerful way to engage users and keep them informed about updates or important events in your app. You can use Flask to implement a backend API for sending push notifications to mobile devices using services like Firebase Cloud Messaging (FCM).

Use Case 3: File Upload and Storage

Many mobile apps require functionality for uploading and storing files, such as images, videos, or documents. Flask can handle file uploads and store them in a filesystem or cloud storage services like Amazon S3 or Google Cloud Storage.

```python
from flask import Flask, request

app = Flask(__name__)

# Upload endpoint
@app.route('/upload', methods=['POST'])
def upload_file():
    if 'file' not in request.files:
        return jsonify({'error': 'No file part'}), 400
```

```
    file = request.files['file']
    if file.filename == '':
        return jsonify({'error': 'No selected file'}), 400
    # Save the file to the desired location
    file.save('/path/to/uploaded/file/' + file.filename)
    return jsonify({'message': 'File uploaded successfully'})

if __name__ == '__main__':
    app.run(debug=True)
```
```

## Use Case 4: Geolocation Services

Integrating geolocation services into your mobile app can enable features such as location-based recommendations, navigation, or social check-ins. Flask APIs can interact with geolocation APIs like Google Maps Geocoding API or OpenStreetMap Nominatim API to provide location-based information to your mobile app.

## Use Case 5: Analytics and Reporting

Collecting and analyzing user data is essential for understanding user behavior and improving your mobile app. Flask APIs can handle data collection from mobile
```

app clients and provide endpoints for generating analytics reports or visualizations using libraries like Matplotlib or Plotly.

In this tutorial, we've explored additional mobile app use cases and demonstrated how to implement them using Flask APIs. From user authentication and push notifications to file upload and geolocation services, Flask provides the flexibility and tools to support various functionalities required by modern mobile apps. By leveraging Flask's simplicity and extensibility, you can build powerful backend APIs to support your mobile app development efforts and create engaging and feature-rich experiences for your users.

Chapter 8

Using Flask Extensions for Enhanced Functionality (Security, Serialization)

Using Flask extensions can greatly enhance the functionality of your APIs, especially in terms of security and serialization. In this tutorial, we'll explore some popular Flask extensions and demonstrate how to integrate them into your API for mobile app development.

1. Flask-Security: User Authentication and Authorization

Flask-Security is an extension that provides authentication, authorization, and user management features to Flask applications. It offers integration with popular authentication methods like username/password, OAuth, and token-based authentication.

```python
from flask import Flask
from flask_security import Security, SQLAlchemyUserDatastore, UserMixin, RoleMixin

app = Flask(__name__)
```

```python
app.config['SECRET_KEY'] = 'your_secret_key'
app.config['SQLALCHEMY_DATABASE_URI'] = 'sqlite:///app.db'

# Define database models
from flask_sqlalchemy import SQLAlchemy
db = SQLAlchemy(app)

roles_users = db.Table('roles_users',
    db.Column('user_id', db.Integer(), db.ForeignKey('user.id')),
    db.Column('role_id', db.Integer(), db.ForeignKey('role.id')))

class Role(db.Model, RoleMixin):
    id = db.Column(db.Integer(), primary_key=True)
    name = db.Column(db.String(80), unique=True)
    description = db.Column(db.String(255))

class User(db.Model, UserMixin):
    id = db.Column(db.Integer, primary_key=True)
    username = db.Column(db.String(255), unique=True)
    password = db.Column(db.String(255))
    roles = db.relationship('Role', secondary=roles_users,
                backref=db.backref('users', lazy='dynamic'))
```

```python
# Setup Flask-Security
user_datastore = SQLAlchemyUserDatastore(db, User, Role)
security = Security(app, user_datastore)

if __name__ == '__main__':
    app.run(debug=True)
```

2. Flask-RESTful: Building RESTful APIs

Flask-RESTful is an extension that adds support for quickly building REST APIs in Flask. It simplifies the process of defining resources, handling request parsing, and serializing responses.

```python
from flask import Flask
from flask_restful import Api, Resource

app = Flask(__name__)
api = Api(app)

class HelloWorld(Resource):
    def get(self):
        return {'message': 'Hello, World!'}
```

```
api.add_resource(HelloWorld, '/')

if __name__ == '__main__':
    app.run(debug=True)
```

3. Flask-JWT-Extended: JSON Web Tokens (JWT) for Authentication

Flask-JWT-Extended is an extension that provides JWT-based authentication for Flask applications. It allows you to protect endpoints and authenticate users using JSON Web Tokens.

```python
from flask import Flask, jsonify
from flask_jwt_extended import JWTManager, jwt_required, create_access_token

app = Flask(__name__)
app.config['JWT_SECRET_KEY'] = 'your_secret_key'

jwt = JWTManager(app)

# Login endpoint
@app.route('/login', methods=['POST'])
def login():
```

```
    # Authenticate user
    access_token = create_access_token(identity='username')
    return jsonify({'access_token': access_token}), 200

# Protected endpoint
@app.route('/protected', methods=['GET'])
@jwt_required()
def protected():
    return jsonify({'message': 'You are authenticated'}), 200

if __name__ == '__main__':
    app.run(debug=True)
```

4. Flask-Marshmallow: Serialization and Deserialization

Flask-Marshmallow is an extension that integrates the Marshmallow library with Flask, providing a convenient way to serialize and deserialize data objects. It helps validate and format data before sending it as a response or receiving it as a request.

```python
from flask import Flask, request, jsonify
```

```python
from flask_marshmallow import Marshmallow

app = Flask(__name__)
ma = Marshmallow(app)

# Define data model
class UserSchema(ma.Schema):
    class Meta:
        fields = ('id', 'username', 'email')

# Create instances of schema
user_schema = UserSchema()
users_schema = UserSchema(many=True)

# Example endpoint for serialization
@app.route('/user', methods=['POST'])
def add_user():
    username = request.json['username']
    email = request.json['email']
    # Validate and serialize data
    new_user = {'id': 1, 'username': username, 'email': email}
    result = user_schema.dump(new_user)
    return jsonify(result), 201

if __name__ == '__main__':
    app.run(debug=True)
```

```

In this tutorial, we've explored some popular Flask extensions for enhancing the functionality of your APIs, especially in terms of security and serialization. By integrating extensions like Flask-Security, Flask-RESTful, Flask-JWT-Extended, and Flask-Marshmallow into your Flask application, you can streamline the development process and build robust APIs to support your mobile app development efforts. These extensions provide powerful features and tools to handle user authentication, build RESTful APIs, implement token-based authentication, and serialize/deserialize data efficiently, making Flask a versatile choice for building backend APIs for mobile apps.

## Working with Asynchronous Tasks and Background Jobs

Working with asynchronous tasks and background jobs in Flask is essential for handling long-running processes without blocking the main application thread. This can include tasks like sending emails, processing data, or performing heavy computations. In this tutorial, we'll explore how to integrate asynchronous tasks and background jobs into a Flask API for mobile app development.
```

Setting Up Flask and Celery:

To work with asynchronous tasks and background jobs in Flask, we'll use Celery, a distributed task queue. First, make sure you have Python and pip installed on your system. Then, install Flask and Celery:

```bash
pip install Flask Celery
```

Next, create a new directory for your project and navigate into it:

```bash
mkdir async_tasks
cd async_tasks
```

Creating the Flask App:

Create a new Python file named `app.py` in your project directory. This file will contain the code for our Flask application.

```python
from flask import Flask
```

```python
from celery import Celery

app = Flask(__name__)

# Configure Celery
app.config['CELERY_BROKER_URL'] = 'redis://localhost:6379/0'
app.config['CELERY_RESULT_BACKEND'] = 'redis://localhost:6379/0'

# Initialize Celery
celery = Celery(app.name, broker=app.config['CELERY_BROKER_URL'])
celery.conf.update(app.config)

# Example asynchronous task
@celery.task
def send_email(email):
    # Simulate sending email
    return f'Email sent to {email}'

if __name__ == '__main__':
    app.run(debug=True)
```

Running a Celery Worker:

To execute Celery tasks asynchronously, you'll need to run a Celery worker. Open a new terminal window and navigate to your project directory. Then, run the following command:

```bash
celery -A app.celery worker --loglevel=info
```

This command starts a Celery worker that listens for tasks and executes them as they're received.

Using Asynchronous Tasks in Flask:

Now, let's create an endpoint in our Flask app to trigger the asynchronous task.

```python
from flask import jsonify

@app.route('/send_email/<email>', methods=['GET'])
def trigger_send_email(email):
    # Trigger the asynchronous task
    send_email.delay(email)
    return jsonify({'message': 'Email sending task queued'})
```

In this tutorial, we've explored how to work with asynchronous tasks and background jobs in Flask using Celery. By integrating Celery into your Flask application, you can offload long-running processes to separate workers, allowing your main application to remain responsive and handle multiple requests efficiently. This is crucial for building scalable and performant APIs to support mobile app development, where tasks like sending emails or processing data may take time and should not block the main application thread. With Celery, you can easily manage and execute asynchronous tasks in your Flask app, enhancing its capabilities and improving user experience.

Leveraging Caching Mechanisms for Improved Performance

Leveraging caching mechanisms in Flask APIs can significantly improve performance by reducing the time required to fetch and process data. Caching involves storing frequently accessed data in memory or a persistent storage mechanism to avoid redundant computations or database queries. In this tutorial, we'll explore how to integrate caching mechanisms into a Flask API for mobile app development.

Setting Up Flask and Flask-Caching:

First, make sure you have Python and pip installed on your system. Then, install Flask and Flask-Caching:

```bash
pip install Flask Flask-Caching
```

Next, create a new directory for your project and navigate into it:

```bash
mkdir caching_example
cd caching_example
```

Creating the Flask App:

Create a new Python file named `app.py` in your project directory. This file will contain the code for our Flask application.

```python
from flask import Flask
from flask_caching import Cache

app = Flask(__name__)
```

```python
# Configure Flask-Caching
app.config['CACHE_TYPE'] = 'simple'
cache = Cache(app)

# Dummy function to simulate expensive computation
def perform_expensive_computation(num):
    result = 0
    for i in range(num):
        result += i
    return result

# Endpoint to perform expensive computation
@app.route('/expensive_computation/<int:num>', methods=['GET'])
@cache.cached(timeout=300)  # Cache the result for 300 seconds
def expensive_computation(num):
    result = perform_expensive_computation(num)
    return f'Result of expensive computation for {num}: {result}'

if __name__ == '__main__':
    app.run(debug=True)
```

Explaining the Code:

We've created a Flask application with an endpoint `/expensive_computation/<num>` that performs an expensive computation and returns the result. We use Flask-Caching to cache the result of the computation for a specified period (300 seconds in this case). Subsequent requests with the same input will be served from the cache instead of recomputing the result.

Testing the Endpoint:

Start the Flask development server by running:

```bash
python app.py
```

Now, open your web browser and navigate to `http://127.0.0.1:5000/expensive_computation/10000`. You should see the result of the expensive computation. Subsequent requests to the same endpoint with the same input will be served from the cache.

In this tutorial, we've explored how to leverage caching mechanisms in Flask APIs using Flask-Caching. By caching frequently accessed data or expensive computations, you can improve the performance of your

API and reduce response times for mobile app clients. Caching is especially useful for scenarios where data is static or changes infrequently, such as reference data or computation results. With Flask-Caching, you can easily integrate caching into your Flask applications and optimize performance to provide a better user experience for mobile app users.

Best Practices for Error Handling and Logging in Flask APIs

Implementing robust error handling and logging mechanisms in Flask APIs is crucial for identifying and resolving issues quickly, improving the reliability and stability of your application. In this tutorial, we'll explore best practices for error handling and logging in Flask APIs and provide code examples to demonstrate their implementation.

Setting Up Flask:

First, make sure you have Python and pip installed on your system. Then, create a new directory for your project and navigate into it:

```bash
mkdir error_handling_logging
cd error_handling_logging
```

```

Install Flask:

```bash
pip install Flask
```

Error Handling:

Flask provides several ways to handle errors, including HTTP error codes, custom error handlers, and error handling middleware.

HTTP Error Codes:

Flask allows you to return specific HTTP status codes to indicate different types of errors. For example, you can return a 404 Not Found error when a resource is not found:

```python
from flask import Flask, jsonify

app = Flask(__name__)

# Endpoint for handling 404 errors
```
```

```python
@app.errorhandler(404)
def not_found_error(error):
    return jsonify({'error': 'Not found'}), 404

if __name__ == '__main__':
    app.run(debug=True)
```

Custom Error Handlers:

You can define custom error handlers to handle specific types of errors and return custom error messages:

```python
# Endpoint for handling custom errors
@app.errorhandler(500)
def internal_server_error(error):
    return jsonify({'error': 'Internal server error'}), 500
```

Error Handling Middleware:

Flask also allows you to register error handling middleware to handle errors globally:

```python
from werkzeug.exceptions import HTTPException
```

```
# Error handling middleware
@app.errorhandler(HTTPException)
def handle_exception(e):
    return jsonify({'error': str(e)}), e.code
```

Logging:

Logging is essential for tracking application behavior, diagnosing issues, and monitoring performance. Flask provides built-in support for logging, allowing you to log messages at different levels of severity.

```python
import logging

# Configure logging
logging.basicConfig(filename='app.log', level=logging.INFO)

# Log a message
logging.info('This is an informational message')
```

Logging Middleware:

You can also register logging middleware to log requests and responses:

```python
from flask import request

# Logging middleware
@app.after_request
def log_request(response):
    app.logger.info(f'{request.method} {request.path} - {response.status_code}')
    return response
```

In this tutorial, we've explored best practices for error handling and logging in Flask APIs. By implementing proper error handling mechanisms and logging strategies, you can enhance the reliability, stability, and maintainability of your Flask applications. Error handling allows you to gracefully handle errors and provide meaningful error messages to clients, while logging helps you track application behavior, diagnose issues, and monitor performance. By following these best practices, you can build robust and resilient Flask APIs to support mobile app development with confidence.

Chapter 9

The Future of Flask Mobile App Development

Emerging Trends in Mobile App Development

The future of Flask mobile app development is influenced by emerging trends in the mobile app development industry. While Flask is primarily known for its use in web development, it can also be leveraged to build robust APIs to support mobile app development. In this section, we'll explore some emerging trends in mobile app development and discuss how Flask APIs can adapt to these trends.

1. Progressive Web Apps (PWAs):

Progressive web apps (PWAs) are web applications that leverage modern web technologies to provide a native app-like experience to users. PWAs offer features such as offline support, push notifications, and installation to the home screen. Flask APIs can serve as the backend for PWAs, providing data and functionality to the frontend web application.

```python
from flask import Flask, jsonify
```

```
app = Flask(__name__)

# Endpoint for serving data to PWA
@app.route('/data', methods=['GET'])
def get_data():
    data = {'message': 'Hello from Flask API'}
    return jsonify(data)

if __name__ == '__main__':
    app.run(debug=True)
```

2. Serverless Architecture:

Serverless architecture, also known as Function as a Service (FaaS), allows developers to build and deploy applications without managing servers. With serverless platforms like AWS Lambda or Google Cloud Functions, Flask APIs can be deployed as serverless functions, reducing operational overhead and scaling costs.

3. GraphQL APIs:

GraphQL is a query language for APIs that enables clients to request only the data they need. Flask can be used to build GraphQL APIs using libraries like Flask-GraphQL, allowing mobile app clients to fetch specific data efficiently over a single HTTP request.

4. Microservices Architecture:

Microservices architecture involves breaking down large applications into smaller, independent services that can be developed, deployed, and scaled independently. Flask APIs are well-suited for building microservices, allowing developers to create focused and modular components that serve specific functionalities to mobile app clients.

```python
from flask import Flask, jsonify

app = Flask(__name__)

# User service endpoint
@app.route('/users/<user_id>', methods=['GET'])
def get_user(user_id):
    # Fetch user data from database
    user_data = {'id': user_id, 'name': 'John Doe'}
    return jsonify(user_data)

if __name__ == '__main__':
```

```
    app.run(debug=True)
```

5. Machine Learning and AI Integration:

Mobile apps are increasingly leveraging machine learning (ML) and artificial intelligence (AI) capabilities to provide personalized experiences and predictive insights to users. Flask APIs can integrate with ML and AI models to serve predictions, recommendations, and insights to mobile app clients.

```python
from flask import Flask, jsonify, request
import numpy as np
import joblib

app = Flask(__name__)

# Load ML model
model = joblib.load('model.pkl')

# Endpoint for making predictions
@app.route('/predict', methods=['POST'])
def predict():
    data = request.json
    features = np.array(data['features']).reshape(1, -1)
```

```
    prediction = model.predict(features)
    return jsonify({'prediction': prediction})

if __name__ == '__main__':
    app.run(debug=True)
```

The future of Flask mobile app development is shaped by emerging trends in the mobile app development industry. As mobile apps evolve to meet the changing needs and expectations of users, Flask APIs can adapt to these trends by embracing technologies like PWAs, serverless architecture, GraphQL, microservices, and machine learning/AI integration. By staying abreast of these trends and leveraging Flask's flexibility and simplicity, developers can build scalable, performance, and feature-rich APIs to support mobile app development effectively.

Integrating Flask APIs with Cloud Services (AWS, Google Cloud)

Integrating Flask APIs with cloud services like AWS (Amazon Web Services) and Google Cloud can provide numerous benefits for mobile app development, including scalability, reliability, and accessibility. In this tutorial, we'll explore how to integrate Flask APIs with

AWS and Google Cloud services and provide code examples to demonstrate their implementation.

Setting Up Flask:

First, make sure you have Python and pip installed on your system. Then, create a new directory for your project and navigate into it:

```bash
mkdir cloud_integration
cd cloud_integration
```

Install Flask:

```bash
pip install Flask
```

Integrating with AWS:

1. AWS Lambda:

AWS Lambda allows you to run code without provisioning or managing servers. You can deploy Flask

APIs as AWS Lambda functions using the `aws-lambda-python` runtime.

```python
# app.py
from flask import Flask

app = Flask(__name__)

@app.route('/')
def hello():
    return 'Hello from Flask running on AWS Lambda!'

if __name__ == '__main__':
    app.run(debug=True)
```

2. Amazon API Gateway:

Amazon API Gateway allows you to create, publish, maintain, monitor, and secure APIs at any scale. You can use API Gateway to expose your Flask APIs as HTTP endpoints.

```python
# app.py
from flask import Flask, jsonify
```

```
app = Flask(__name__)

@app.route('/data')
def get_data():
    data = {'message': 'Hello from Flask API on AWS'}
    return jsonify(data)

if __name__ == '__main__':
    app.run(debug=True)
```

Integrating with Google Cloud:

1. Google Cloud Functions:

Google Cloud Functions allows you to run event-driven serverless functions in Google Cloud. You can deploy Flask APIs as Google Cloud Functions using the `functions-framework` runtime.

```python
# app.py
from flask import Flask, jsonify

app = Flask(__name__)
```

```python
@app.route('/data')
def get_data():
    data = {'message': 'Hello from Flask API on Google Cloud'}
    return jsonify(data)

if __name__ == '__main__':
    app.run(debug=True)
```

2. Google Cloud Endpoints:

Google Cloud Endpoints allows you to create, deploy, and manage APIs on Google Cloud. You can use Cloud Endpoints to expose your Flask APIs as HTTP endpoints with built-in security, monitoring, and logging.

```python
# app.py
from flask import Flask, jsonify

app = Flask(__name__)

@app.route('/data')
def get_data():
    data = {'message': 'Hello from Flask API on Google Cloud Endpoints'}
```

```
    return jsonify(data)

if __name__ == '__main__':
    app.run(debug=True)
```

Integrating Flask APIs with cloud services like AWS and Google Cloud can provide numerous benefits for mobile app development, including scalability, reliability, and accessibility. By leveraging AWS Lambda, Amazon API Gateway, Google Cloud Functions, and Google Cloud Endpoints, you can deploy Flask APIs as serverless functions and expose them as HTTP endpoints with built-in security, monitoring, and logging capabilities. This allows you to focus on building and maintaining your Flask APIs while taking advantage of the infrastructure and services provided by cloud providers to support mobile app development effectively.

Continuous Integration and Continuous Delivery (CI/CD) for Flask Apps

Continuous Integration and Continuous Delivery (CI/CD) are essential practices in modern software development workflows, including Flask app development. CI/CD helps automate and streamline the process of building, testing, and deploying Flask apps, leading to faster delivery of high-quality software. In this tutorial, we'll explore how to set up CI/CD pipelines for Flask apps using popular tools like GitHub Actions.

Setting Up a Flask App:

First, create a new directory for your Flask app and navigate into it:

```bash
mkdir flask_cicd
cd flask_cicd
```

Initialize a new Python virtual environment and install Flask:

```bash
python -m venv venv
source venv/bin/activate
pip install Flask
```

Create a new file named `app.py` and add a simple Flask app:

```python
# app.py
```

```python
from flask import Flask

app = Flask(__name__)

@app.route('/')
def hello():
    return 'Hello, World!'

if __name__ == '__main__':
    app.run(debug=True)
```

Setting Up a GitHub Repository:

Create a new GitHub repository for your Flask app and push your code to it:

```bash
git init
git add .
git commit -m "Initial commit"
git remote add origin <repository_url>
git push -u origin master
```

Setting Up Continuous Integration (CI) with GitHub Actions:

Create a new directory named `.github/workflows` in your project directory:

```bash
mkdir -p .github/workflows
```

Inside the `.github/workflows` directory, create a new YAML file named `ci.yml` and add the following configuration:

```yaml
# .github/workflows/ci.yml
name: CI

on:
  push:
    branches:
      - master
  pull_request:
    branches:
      - master

jobs:
  build:
    runs-on: ubuntu-latest
```

```yaml
    steps:
    - uses: actions/checkout@v2

    - name: Set up Python
      uses: actions/setup-python@v2
      with:
        python-version: '3.8'

    - name: Install dependencies
      run: |
        python -m pip install --upgrade pip
        pip install -r requirements.txt

    - name: Lint with Flake8
      run: |
        pip install flake8
        flake8 .

    - name: Test with pytest
      run: |
        pip install pytest
        pytest
```

This configuration sets up a CI pipeline that runs on every push to the `master` branch. It installs dependencies, lints the code with Flake8, and runs tests with pytest.

Setting Up Continuous Delivery (CD) with GitHub Actions:

To set up CD, we'll use GitHub Actions to deploy our Flask app to a cloud platform like Heroku. First, make sure you have a Heroku account and the Heroku CLI installed.

Inside the `.github/workflows` directory, create a new YAML file named `cd.yml` and add the following configuration:

```yaml
# .github/workflows/cd.yml
name: CD

on:
  push:
    branches:
      - master

jobs:
  deploy:
    runs-on: ubuntu-latest
```

```
steps:
- uses: actions/checkout@v2

- name: Set up Python
  uses: actions/setup-python@v2
  with:
    python-version: '3.8'

- name: Install Heroku CLI
  run: |
    curl https://cli-assets.heroku.com/install.sh | sh

- name: Login to Heroku
  run: heroku login -i

- name: Create Heroku app
  run: heroku create

- name: Deploy to Heroku
  run: git push heroku master
```

This configuration sets up a CD pipeline that deploys the Flask app to Heroku on every push to the `master` branch.

In this tutorial, we've explored how to set up CI/CD pipelines for Flask apps using GitHub Actions. CI helps automate the process of building, testing, and linting the code, ensuring its quality. CD automates the process of deploying the Flask app to a cloud platform like Heroku, making it easier to deliver updates to users quickly and reliably. By integrating CI/CD into your Flask app development workflow, you can ensure high-quality code and streamline the deployment process, leading to faster delivery of features and improvements to your mobile app.

Staying Updated: Resources for Flask Developers

Staying updated as a Flask developer is crucial for keeping up with the latest trends, best practices, and tools in the Flask ecosystem. Fortunately, there are plenty of resources available to help you stay informed and continuously improve your skills. In this guide, we'll explore some of the top resources for Flask developers, including documentation, tutorials, blogs, forums, and community events.

1. Official Flask Documentation:

The official Flask documentation is an invaluable resource for Flask developers. It provides comprehensive guides, tutorials, and references on Flask's features, APIs, and extensions. Whether you're a beginner or an experienced developer, the Flask documentation is a must-read resource for learning and mastering Flask.

```python
from flask import Flask

app = Flask(__name__)

@app.route('/')
def hello():
    return 'Hello, World!'

if __name__ == '__main__':
    app.run(debug=True)
```

2. Flask Mega-Tutorial:

The Flask Mega-Tutorial by Miguel Grinberg is a comprehensive guide to building web applications with Flask. It covers everything from setting up a development environment to deploying a production-ready application. The tutorial is divided into multiple chapters, each focusing on a different aspect of Flask development, making it easy to follow and learn at your own pace.

3. Flask-Blog:

The Flask-Blog is a community-driven blog that covers a wide range of topics related to Flask development. It features tutorials, articles, and tips from experienced Flask developers, providing insights and best practices for building Flask applications. You can also contribute your own articles and share your knowledge with the community.

4. Flask Reddit:

The Flask subreddit is a popular online community for Flask developers to share news, tutorials, and discussions related to Flask development. It's a great place to ask questions, seek advice, and connect with other Flask enthusiasts. The subreddit also hosts regular Flask-related events, such as AMAs (Ask Me Anything) with Flask experts.

5. Flask Extensions:

Flask has a rich ecosystem of extensions that provide additional functionality and features for Flask applications. The Flask Extensions Registry is a centralized repository of Flask extensions, where you can discover and explore various extensions to enhance your Flask projects. Some popular Flask extensions include Flask-SQLAlchemy, Flask-RESTful, Flask-JWT-Extended, and Flask-WTF.

```python
from flask import Flask
from flask_sqlalchemy import SQLAlchemy

app = Flask(__name__)
app.config['SQLALCHEMY_DATABASE_URI'] = 'sqlite:///app.db'
db = SQLAlchemy(app)

class User(db.Model):
    id = db.Column(db.Integer, primary_key=True)
    username = db.Column(db.String(80), unique=True, nullable=False)
    email = db.Column(db.String(120), unique=True, nullable=False)

    def __repr__(self):
        return '<User %r>' % self.username

if __name__ == '__main__':
```

```
    app.run(debug=True)
```

6. Flask Conferences and Meetups:

Attending Flask conferences, meetups, and workshops is a great way to network with other Flask developers, learn from experts, and stay updated on the latest developments in the Flask community. Events like PyCon, FlaskCon, and local Flask meetups offer opportunities to connect with like-minded individuals and gain valuable insights into Flask development.

Staying updated as a Flask developer is essential for keeping pace with the rapidly evolving landscape of web development. By leveraging resources like the official Flask documentation, tutorials, blogs, forums, and community events, you can continue to enhance your skills, stay informed about the latest trends and best practices, and contribute to the vibrant Flask community. Whether you're a beginner or an experienced developer, there's always something new to learn and explore in the world of Flask development.

Conclusion

In conclusion, Flask API development for mobile apps offers a versatile and efficient way to build robust backend services that power modern mobile applications. Throughout this journey, we've delved into the intricacies of Flask, exploring its flexibility, simplicity, and scalability, as well as its integration with various tools, libraries, and cloud services. From setting up a basic Flask app to implementing advanced features like authentication, serialization, and asynchronous tasks, we've covered a wide range of topics to help you become proficient in Flask API development for mobile app development.

Flask's lightweight and minimalist design make it an ideal choice for building APIs that serve data and functionality to mobile app clients. Its modular architecture allows developers to create modular and maintainable codebases, while its extensive ecosystem of extensions provides additional features and functionalities to enhance the capabilities of Flask applications. Whether you're building a simple RESTful API or a complex microservices architecture, Flask empowers you to create scalable and performant backend services that meet the demands of modern mobile app development.

As we've seen, Flask integrates seamlessly with various technologies and platforms, including cloud services like AWS and Google Cloud, CI/CD tools like GitHub Actions, and frontend frameworks like React Native and Flutter. By leveraging these tools and technologies, Flask developers can streamline the development, testing, and deployment processes, leading to faster delivery of high-quality mobile applications. Additionally, staying updated with resources like official documentation, tutorials, blogs, forums, and community events is essential for keeping pace with the latest trends and best practices in Flask API development.

In the ever-evolving landscape of mobile app development, Flask continues to play a vital role as a reliable and efficient framework for building backend services. Its simplicity, flexibility, and scalability make it an attractive choice for developers looking to create powerful APIs that support mobile app development. Whether you're a beginner exploring Flask for the first time or an experienced developer looking to expand your skills, Flask offers a wealth of opportunities to build innovative and impactful mobile applications that delight users and drive business success.

In conclusion, Flask API development for mobile app development is not just about building backend services—it's about creating experiences that connect with users, empower businesses, and drive digital innovation. With Flask as your toolkit, the possibilities are endless, and the journey is bound to be exciting and rewarding. So, embrace Flask, explore its capabilities, and embark on a journey of creativity, collaboration, and continuous learning in the dynamic world of mobile app development.

Appendix

Glossary of terms

Here's a glossary of terms commonly used in Flask API development for mobile app development:

1. Flask: Flask is a micro web framework written in Python. It is lightweight and easy to use, making it an ideal choice for building web APIs to support mobile app development.

2. API (Application Programming Interface): An API is a set of rules and protocols that allows different software applications to communicate with each other. In the context of Flask, an API refers to the endpoints and methods exposed by a Flask application for interacting with mobile app clients.

3. Endpoint: An endpoint is a specific URL within a web API that corresponds to a particular resource or action. In Flask, endpoints are defined using route decorators, such as `@app.route('/')`, to specify the URL and associated function.

4. HTTP Methods: HTTP methods, also known as HTTP verbs, are used to indicate the desired action to be performed on a resource. Common HTTP methods include GET (retrieve data), POST (create new data), PUT (update existing data), DELETE (remove data), and PATCH (partially update data). In Flask, HTTP methods are handled using route decorators, such as `@app.route('/', methods=['GET'])`.

5. JSON (JavaScript Object Notation): JSON is a lightweight data-interchange format that is easy for humans to read and write, and easy for machines to parse and generate. In Flask API development, JSON is commonly used for exchanging data between the server and mobile app clients.

6. Serialization: Serialization is the process of converting complex data structures, such as objects or dictionaries, into a format that can be easily transmitted over a network, such as JSON. In Flask, serialization is often performed using libraries like Flask-RESTful or Flask-Marshmallow.

7. Deserialization: Deserialization is the process of converting serialized data back into its original form. In Flask, deserialization is often performed when receiving data from mobile app clients and converting it into Python objects or dictionaries.

8. Authentication: Authentication is the process of verifying the identity of a user or application. In Flask API development, authentication is commonly implemented using techniques like token-based authentication or OAuth.

9. Authorization: Authorization is the process of determining whether a user or application has permission to access a particular resource or perform a particular action. In Flask API development, authorization is often implemented using techniques like role-based access control (RBAC) or permissions.

10. Middleware: Middleware is software that acts as a bridge between an application and the underlying operating system or other software components. In Flask, middleware can be used to perform tasks like logging, error handling, or request/response modification.

11. CORS (Cross-Origin Resource Sharing): CORS is a security feature implemented by web browsers to restrict cross-origin HTTP requests initiated from scripts. In Flask API development, CORS headers can be added to responses to allow or restrict access from different origins.

12. Deployment: Deployment is the process of making a Flask application accessible to users over the internet. This often involves configuring a web server, such as Nginx or Apache, and deploying the Flask application using tools like Gunicorn or uWSGI.

This glossary provides a basic understanding of key terms and concepts in Flask API development for mobile app development. By familiarizing yourself with these terms, you'll be better equipped to navigate the world of Flask development and build powerful backend services to support your mobile applications.

Essential Flask Resources and Libraries

Flask, a lightweight and versatile web framework for Python, offers a rich ecosystem of resources and libraries to simplify and enhance Flask API development for mobile app development. In this guide, we'll explore some essential Flask resources and libraries, along with code examples demonstrating their usage in mobile app development.

1. Flask-SQLAlchemy:

Flask-SQLAlchemy is a Flask extension that provides integration with SQLAlchemy, a powerful SQL toolkit and Object-Relational Mapping (ORM) library for Python. SQLAlchemy allows developers to interact with relational databases using Python objects, making database operations more intuitive and efficient.

```python
from flask import Flask
from flask_sqlalchemy import SQLAlchemy

app = Flask(__name__)
app.config['SQLALCHEMY_DATABASE_URI'] = 'sqlite:///app.db'
db = SQLAlchemy(app)
```

```python
class User(db.Model):
    id = db.Column(db.Integer, primary_key=True)
    username = db.Column(db.String(80), unique=True, nullable=False)
    email = db.Column(db.String(120), unique=True, nullable=False)

    def __repr__(self):
        return '<User %r>' % self.username

if __name__ == '__main__':
    app.run(debug=True)
```

2. Flask-RESTful:

Flask-RESTful is an extension for Flask that adds support for building RESTful APIs quickly and easily. It provides tools for defining resources, handling requests, and serializing/deserializing data in JSON format, making it a popular choice for building APIs to support mobile app development.

```python
from flask import Flask
from flask_restful import Api, Resource
```

```python
app = Flask(__name__)
api = Api(app)

class HelloWorld(Resource):
    def get(self):
        return {'message': 'Hello, World!'}

api.add_resource(HelloWorld, '/')

if __name__ == '__main__':
    app.run(debug=True)
```

3. Flask-JWT-Extended:

Flask-JWT-Extended is an extension for Flask that adds support for JSON Web Tokens (JWT) authentication. JWT authentication is commonly used in mobile app development to secure APIs and authenticate users, providing a stateless and secure way to manage user sessions.

```python
from flask import Flask
from flask_jwt_extended import JWTManager, jwt_required, create_access_token
```

```
app = Flask(__name__)
app.config['JWT_SECRET_KEY'] = 'super-secret'  # Change this to a random secret key
jwt = JWTManager(app)

@app.route('/login', methods=['POST'])
def login():
    # Authenticate user
    access_token = create_access_token(identity='user_id')
    return {'access_token': access_token}

@app.route('/protected', methods=['GET'])
@jwt_required()
def protected():
    return {'message': 'Protected endpoint'}

if __name__ == '__main__':
    app.run(debug=True)
```
```

### 4. Flask-CORS:

Flask-CORS is an extension for Flask that adds support for Cross-Origin Resource Sharing (CORS), allowing you to control access to your API from different origins.
```

CORS headers can be added to responses to allow or restrict access from specific domains, making it a useful tool for securing APIs in mobile app development.

```python
from flask import Flask
from flask_cors import CORS

app = Flask(__name__)
CORS(app)

@app.route('/')
def hello():
    return 'Hello, World!'

if __name__ == '__main__':
    app.run(debug=True)
```

5. Flask-Marshmallow:

Flask-Marshmallow is an extension for Flask that provides integration with Marshmallow, a powerful library for object serialization and deserialization. Marshmallow allows you to define schemas for your data models and easily serialize/deserialize them to/from

JSON format, making it a valuable tool for handling data in Flask APIs.

```python
from flask import Flask
from flask_marshmallow import Marshmallow
from marshmallow import fields

app = Flask(__name__)
ma = Marshmallow(app)

class UserSchema(ma.Schema):
    id = fields.Int()
    username = fields.Str()
    email = fields.Email()

user_schema = UserSchema()

if __name__ == '__main__':
    app.run(debug=True)
```

Flask offers a rich ecosystem of resources and libraries to simplify and enhance Flask API development for mobile app development. From database integration and RESTful API support to authentication and data serialization, these essential Flask resources and libraries provide the tools and functionality you need to build powerful and scalable APIs to support your mobile applications. By leveraging these resources and libraries, you can streamline your development process, improve code quality, and deliver high-quality mobile apps that meet the needs of your users.

Common Flask API Development Pitfalls and Solutions

Flask API development for mobile app development offers flexibility and scalability, but it also comes with its own set of challenges and pitfalls. In this guide, we'll explore some common Flask API development pitfalls and provide solutions to address them, along with code examples to demonstrate best practices.

Pitfall 1: Poor Error Handling

One of the most common pitfalls in Flask API development is poor error handling. Failing to handle errors properly can lead to unexpected behavior and security vulnerabilities in your API.

Solution:

Implement robust error handling mechanisms to catch and handle errors gracefully. Use Flask's `@app.errorhandler` decorator to define custom error handlers for different HTTP error codes.

```python
from flask import Flask, jsonify
```

```
app = Flask(__name__)

@app.errorhandler(404)
def not_found_error(error):
    return jsonify({'error': 'Not found'}), 404

@app.errorhandler(500)
def internal_server_error(error):
    return jsonify({'error': 'Internal server error'}), 500

if __name__ == '__main__':
    app.run(debug=True)
```
```

## Pitfall 2: Lack of Authentication and Authorization

Securing your Flask API is crucial to protect sensitive data and prevent unauthorized access. Failing to implement authentication and authorization mechanisms can leave your API vulnerable to security breaches.

**Solution**:

Implement authentication and authorization using techniques like token-based authentication or OAuth. Use Flask-JWT-Extended to add JWT authentication to
```

your API, and Flask-Principal for role-based access control (RBAC).

```python
from flask import Flask
from flask_jwt_extended import JWTManager, jwt_required, create_access_token

app = Flask(__name__)
app.config['JWT_SECRET_KEY'] = 'super-secret'  # Change this to a random secret key
jwt = JWTManager(app)

@app.route('/login', methods=['POST'])
def login():
    # Authenticate user
    access_token = create_access_token(identity='user_id')
    return {'access_token': access_token}

@app.route('/protected', methods=['GET'])
@jwt_required()
def protected():
    return {'message': 'Protected endpoint'}

if __name__ == '__main__':
    app.run(debug=True)
```

```

## Pitfall 3: Inefficient Database Queries

Inefficient database queries can lead to poor performance and scalability issues in your Flask API. Failing to optimize database queries can result in slow response times and degraded user experience.

**Solution**:

Optimize database queries by using indexes, caching, and pagination. Use SQLAlchemy's query optimization techniques like `filter()` and `join()` to retrieve only the data you need, and avoid making unnecessary database calls.

```python
from flask import Flask
from flask_sqlalchemy import SQLAlchemy

app = Flask(__name__)
app.config['SQLALCHEMY_DATABASE_URI'] = 'sqlite:///app.db'
db = SQLAlchemy(app)

class User(db.Model):

```
    id = db.Column(db.Integer, primary_key=True)
    username = db.Column(db.String(80), unique=True, nullable=False)
    email = db.Column(db.String(120), unique=True, nullable=False)

    def __repr__(self):
        return '<User %r>' % self.username

if __name__ == '__main__':
    app.run(debug=True)
```

Pitfall 4: Lack of Input Validation

Failing to validate input data can lead to security vulnerabilities and data integrity issues in your Flask API. Without proper input validation, your API may be susceptible to injection attacks, data manipulation, and other forms of exploitation.

Solution:

Implement input validation using libraries like Flask-WTF or Marshmallow. Use validators and sanitizers to validate and sanitize input data before processing it, and handle validation errors gracefully.

```python
from flask import Flask, request
from wtforms import Form, StringField, validators

app = Flask(__name__)

class LoginForm(Form):
    username = StringField('Username', validators=[validators.DataRequired()])
    password = StringField('Password', validators=[validators.DataRequired()])

@app.route('/login', methods=['POST'])
def login():
    form = LoginForm(request.form)
    if form.validate():
        # Process login
        return {'message': 'Login successful'}
    else:
        return {'error': form.errors}, 400

if __name__ == '__main__':
    app.run(debug=True)
```

Flask API development for mobile app development comes with its own set of challenges and pitfalls, but with careful planning and attention to best practices, these challenges can be overcome. By implementing robust error handling, authentication and authorization mechanisms, efficient database queries, and input validation, you can build secure, scalable, and reliable Flask APIs to support your mobile applications. Remember to stay updated with the latest developments in Flask API development and continuously improve your skills to stay ahead of potential pitfalls and ensure the success of your projects.

www.ingramcontent.com/pod-product-compliance
Lightning Source LLC
Chambersburg PA
CBHW031606210526
45464CB00004B/1450